FAMOUS CASES

OF

CIRCUMSTANTIAL EVIDENCE.

WITH AN INTRODUCTION

ON THE

THEORY OF PRESUMPTIVE PROOF:

BY

S. N. PHILLIPS,

AUTHOR OF "PHILLIPS ON EVIDENCE."

BOSTON:

ESTES & LAURIAT.

1873.

CONTENTS.

THE THEORY

OF

PRESUMPTIVE PROOF.

THERE is no branch of legal knowledge which is of more general utility, than that which regards the rules of evidence. The first point in every trial, is to establish the facts of the case; for he who fails in his proof, fails in every thing. Although the jurists hold the law to be always fixed and certain, yet the discovery of the fact, they say, may deceive the most skillful. No work has as yet appeared in the English language on the theory of evidence; and the nature of circumstantial evidence has been still less inquired into. The object of the present Essay is to inquire into some of the more general principles of legal proof, and particularly into that species of proof which is founded on presumptions, and is known to the English lawyer by the name of circumstantial evidence.

Evidence and proof are often confounded, as implying the same idea; but they differ, as cause and effect. Proof is the legal credence which the law gives to any statement, by witnesses or writings; evidence is the legal process by which that proof is made. Hence, we say, that the law admits of no proof but such as is made agreeably to its own principles.

The principles of evidence are founded on our observations on human conduct, on common life, and living manners: they are not just because they are rules of law; but they are rules of law because they are just and reasonable.

It has been found, from common observation, that certain circumstances warrant certain presumptions. Thus, that a mother shall feel an affection for her child,—that a man shall be influenced by his interest,—that youth shall be susceptible of the passion of love,—are laws of our general nature, and grounds of evidence in every country. Of the two women who contended for their right to the child, she was declared to be the mother who would not consent to its being divided betwixt them. When *Lothario* tells us that he stole alone, at night, into the chamber of his mistress, "hot with the Tuscan grape, and high in blood!" *Cætera quis nescit?*

As the principles of evidence are founded on the observations of what we have seen, or believed to have been passing in real life, they will accordingly be suited to the state of the society, in which we live, or to the manners and habits of the times. The following passage, in the excellent memoirs of *Philip de Comines*, I believe to be perfectly true, because it is confirmed by other accounts of the general state of manners at the period when he wrote.

Louis XI. distributed, he asserts, for corrupt purposes, sixteen thousand crowns among the King of England's officers that were about his person, particularly to the chancellor, the master of the rolls, the lord chancellor, &c.*

The truth of this narrative has never been called in question, because it is given by an historian of great gravity and character, and is illustrated by the manners of the age; yet although the author says that his design in writing of these transactions, is to show the method and conduct of all human affairs, by the reading of which such persons as are employed in the negotiation of great matters, may be instructed how to manage their administrations, we should find it difficult to give credence to such facts, if related of any modern lord high chancellor or officer of state of the court of England. Thus, the same presumptive evidence that is good as to the court of Edward IV. and the era of 1477, is altogether extravagant if applied to the court of George III. and the beginning of the 19th century.

* V. 2. p. 7.

The oration of Cicero for Cluentius, exhibits evidence of judicial corruption which can only be credited from our general knowledge of Roman manners at the era of the facts which he describes.

The King of Siam gave credence to everything which a European ambassador told him, as to the circumstances and condition of Europe. until he came to acquaint him, that the rivers and sea were occasionally made so hard, by the cold, that people could walk on them; but this story he totally disbelieved and rejected, as entirely repugnant to every thing which he had either seen or heard; and the ground of his disbelief was perfectly rational.

A similar principle sways our belief in respect to the acts of individuals, as arising in the society and period in which we live. We always refer the credibility of the case to what has fallen within our own observation and experience of men and things. We readily give credence to acts of common occurrence, and are slow in yielding our assent to the existence of new and unlooked for events. When a wretch, at no distant period, in affluent circumstances, was accused of having stolen some sheets of paper in a shop, the judges admitted him to bail against evidence, because the charge was altogether unlikely in one of his condition in life. From these instances, we may safely infer that the principles for our believing or disbelieving any fact, are rather governed by the manners and habits of society, than by any positive rule. The writers on the general law of evidence, such as Mascardus and Menochius, have accordingly declared that all proof is arbitrary, and depends on the feelings of the judges.

There are two species of presumptive proof: the first is the presumption of the law, and the second the presumption of the judge, juryman, or trier.

The presumption of the law is that conclusion which the law attaches to a certain species of guilt. Thus, that he who has deliberately and willfully killed another, has done so from malice, is a presumption of the law. But how far he who has been found with the sword in his hand by the body of the man just killed, did or did not give the mortal stroke, is a presumption to be made by the jury, and is not determinable by any positive rule of law.

The presumption of the law, Montesquieu observes, is preferable to that of man. The French law considers every act of a merchant, during the ten days preceding his bankruptcy, as fraudulent; this is the presumption of the law.

The modern French code has wisely decreed, that when the law, on account of circumstances, shall have deemed certain acts fraudulent, proof shall not be admitted that they were done without fraud. And in our own, as in every other system of legislation, a variety of qualities are presumed as to different persons and things, against which no proof shall be allowed. Certainty is the great object of legislation, and nothing could be established but by the determination of some thing as already fixed.

All proof is in reference to some fact already known and admitted,—what is doubtful must be proved in reference to what is true.

The following rules, by Quintilian, proceed upon this principle, but they are, perhaps, rather curious than useful:—*One thing is, because another is not:* it is day, therefore it is not night. *One thing is, therefore another is:* the sun is risen, therefore it is day. *One thing is not, therefore another is:* it is not night, therefore it is day. *One thing is not, therefore another is not:* he is not rational, therefore not a man.

Evidence is divided into positive and presumptive. Positive evidence is where the witness swears distinctly to the commission of the act or crime which forms the subject of the trial. Presumptive evidence is that conclusion which the jury draw for themselves, from circumstances or minor facts, as sworn to by the witnesses.

Presumptions are consequences drawn from a fact that is known to serve for the discovery of the truth of a fact that is uncertain, and which one seeks to prove. But no presumption can be made but on a fact already known and ascertained. Thus, if the stains of blood on the coat of one tried for murder, are to be presumed as evidence of his guilt, the fact of the stains being occasioned by blood must be first distinctly ascertained; the one presumption cannot be made to aid the other.

The stains are not to be presumed from blood because he is presumed to have been the murderer; nor, on the other hand, is he to be believed the murderer, because the stains are believed to be from blood; for this is reasoning in a circle, and returning back to the point whence the argument commenced. In laws, the arguments should be drawn from one reality to another, and not from reality to figure, or from figure to reality.

Whilst dwelling on the general head of proof, it may be proper to inquire in what does proof naturally consist. Is one witness, according to the principles of natural reason, sufficient to give legal credence, or are two witnesses necessary?

The Roman or civil law has required two witnesses to each separate fact.

But this principle did not, perhaps, arise from the dictates of legal prudence, but was borrowed from a text of Scripture: "In the mouth of two or three shall the truth be established." The text was meant merely to carry reference to certain circumstances incident to the Christian religion. But the principles of religion are happily founded on higher evidence than is necessary to guide men in the business of common life.

The incidents of commerce, and the daily intercourse of mankind require not only that moral certainty which we are warranted, from general observations, to confide in. It were superfluous to show how difficult it must be, nay, how impossible, often, to prove a crime by two witnesses. The absurdity and inconveniency of the rule has been attended with that effect which will always attend an inconvenient law; a variety of shifts have been invented to evade it. One witness is held sufficient to a fact of a general nature, and half proofs have been established.

If the rules of evidence are founded on the principles of human nature; if, like other rules, their fitness is to be judged of by their practical utility, it must be admitted that a proof by one witness, or by circumstances, in certain cases, is good and reasonable.

It is true, that by the English law of high treason, that is, by the 25th of Edward the Third, two witnesses are required to convict a prisoner of the charge: that is to say, one witness to one fact, and another to a different fact, of the same species of treason, shall be held to be two witnesses within the meaning of the statute. But this law was passed for the security of the subject, and to guard against the overbearing influence of the crown in state prosecutions; and it is no doubt in reference to crimes against the state, that Montesquieu has made the following observation:—"Those laws which condemn a man to death, on the deposition of a single witness, are fatal to liberty. In right reason there should be two; because a witness who affirms, and the accused who denies, make an equal balance, and a third must incline the scale."*—Besides, the observation is made by a writer speaking in reference no doubt to the *civil law*, where there is no jury to estimate the weight due to the evidence. In the present Essay, it is not meant to inquire, what crimes should be liable to the punishment of death, and what not; it is only proposed to inquire, what degree of proof is sufficient to satisfy the mind of the commission of the act. The principle in law is clear, that the guilt is neither increased nor diminished by the fullness or defect of the proof.

When, it will be asked, shall a proof be said to complete? The answer must be,—when the judges are satisfied; if the

* Spirit of Laws, b. 12, c. 3.

process be regular. For what is implied by the term to prove?

The jurists acquaint us, that to prove is to convince the judge.

Probare est fidem facere judici. And this is the meaning assigned to the term by the English language. The common saying, as used in argument, where a fact is disputed,—*I will prove this to you,—I will convince you of this,—I will satisfy you on this head,*—sufficiently show, that to prove, only implies, to convince another of the truth of our assertions.

The proof must be held to be complete, on the part of the prosecutor, when he produces the best evidence which the case will afford, and such as shall induce the judges to believe the commission of the fact, until it is refuted by opposite evidence on the part of the defendant:* one story is good, until another is told. Where the evidence is believed, and is sufficient to account for the fact, no other proof is necessary.

Hypothetical reasonings are susceptible of the highest degree of evidence, when the *hypothesis* explains many *phenomena*, and contradicts none; and, when every other *hypothesis* is inconsistent with some of the *phenomena*. And this is the principle on which the philosophy of Sir Isaac Newton, as to the motion of the heavenly bodies, is founded.

Where there is no reason, *not* to believe; that, alone, is a reason for believing the evidence of our senses.

The senses are ever true, but the understanding often reasons ill. It is not proper to reject a probable opinion, without establishing a better in the room of it.

But these remarks are, after all, but barren generalities; and the observation of the great writers on this subject, will too often be found to be just,—that all proof is arbitrary, and cannot be reduced to positive rules. It happens, sometimes,

* Indeed, the proof is complete, on the part of the prosecution, when the best evidence has been produced. That is to say, the proof should be made to rest there, whatever the probable effect of the evidence on the court may or may not be.

that the most probable things are false; for, if they were always separated from falsehood, they would be certain, and not probable. Or, as rendered by some other translators,—

The most probable things, sometimes prove false; because, if they were exempt from falsity, they would not be probable, but certain.*

It is likely several things may happen, which are not likely.

The ancient Romans were so sensible of the uncertainty of evidence, and the difficulty of always ascertaining the guilt of the prisoner, that their form of judgment (or verdict of the jury as we should style it), merely expressed, that he appeared to have done it, *fecisse videtur.*

It is not the fact, always, that constitutes the guilt, but the opinion of the judge. "What have the laws ordered in such a case?" was asked of an advocate of Byzantium: "What I please," was the answer.†

The end of a proof, is to establish the matter in debate. In every case, whether by direct proof, or by that of circumstantial evidence, the jury ought always to be fully satisfied of the guilt of the prisoner, before they return such a verdict. It is immaterial what the proof is, if it is not believed, and brings conviction to the mind of the jury.

It has been, of late years, a favorite theme, to descant upon the certainty of circumstantial evidence. The practice of the law, like other things, has its prejudices; and the name of an eminent man, the success of a particular trial, will sometimes give sanction to a false theory.

Circumstances, it is said, cannot lie. This is very true; but witnesses can. And from whom do you obtain circumstances, but from witnesses? Thus, you are liable to two deceptions: first, in the tale told by the witness; and, secondly, in your own application of those circumstances. Where a fact is positively sworn to, as seen by the witness, the conclusion

* Aristotle, Vide Bayle Dict. Agathon.

† Travels of Anacharsis, v. 4. p. 400.

or inference to be drawn from it, is generally obvious. But, where the inference is to be drawn from a long train of circumstances, it is a matter of judgment; it is an exercise of the understanding; and, as all men do not understand alike, very opposite conclusions are sometimes drawn from the same shades of probability.

When the ancient prudence of the law denied to a prisoner the benefit of counsel, on a capital charge, to plead for him, it was understood that the proof should be so clear, as to be self-evident to the jury. It was understood that the judge should be counsel for the prisoner; that is to say, that he should see that the process was fair and regular, and that no undue advantages were taken; but that process is vitiated in its vital part, when a false principle is introduced.

"A presumption, which necessarily arises from circumstances, is very often more convincing, and more satisfactory, than any other kind of evidence; it is not within the reach and compass of human abilities to invent a train of circumstances, which shall be so connected together as to amount to a proof of guilt, without affording opportunities of contradicting a great part, if not all, of these circumstances." (*Charge of Mr. Justice Bullen, on the trial of Captain Donnellan.*)

I deny the position. I maintain, that the theory is repugnant to the received principles of jurisprudence; as known to the best foreign writers on the law of evidence. I maintain, that it is not warranted by experience,—the greatest proof of every rule, the proof of proofs. And I may further assert, that it is new to the practice of the English law.

First, I shall show, that the theory is repugnant to the received principles of jurisprudence, as known to the best foreign writers, on the law of evidence.

The first to whom I shall refer is Mascardus, a writer of great eminence on the general theory of proof; regarding which, he has published four volumes.

"Proof by evidence of the thing, is superior to every other;

and of all different kinds, none is so great as that which is made by witnesses deposing to what they have seen."*

"Proof by presumption and conjectures," he observes in another place, "cannot be called a true and proper proof."†

The work of Menochius is entirely dedicated to the doctrine of presumptions or circumstantial evidence; and although he displays the partiality for this species of proof, which is natural to one who has dedicated his attention to a particular subject, yet, in the very first chapter of his work, he observes, that "the proof or credence which arises from the testimony of witnesses, is superior to any other."‡

I shall not think it necessary to load this Essay with quotations from other writers on the civil law; the above two possess the most eminent authority of any on the subject of evidence. But the same opinion is expressed by every other author, whom I have had occusion to consult: no one has maintained the absurd position, that circumstances cannot lie; or, that conjectural proof is superior to that of ocular demonstration.

Secondly. I maintain, that it is not warranted by experience,—the great test of every rule.

It might appear invidious, to carry reference to cases of modern occurrence, where fatal mistakes have been discovered of persons too hastily convicted on mere circumstantial evidence; the history of the judicial proceedings in this and every other country will afford too many illustrations.

Some cases of this kind will be found well illustrated in Lord Chief Justice Hale's Pleas of the Crown, vol. 2, p. 289.

Various instances occur, of the fatal error being too late

* Probatio per evidentiam rei omnibus est potentior, et inter omnes ejus generis major est illa, quæ fit per testes de visu. (Macardus de Probationibus, v. 1, q. 3, n. 8.

† Probatio per presumtiones et conjectures dici non potest vera et propria probatio.

‡ Probatio seu fides quæ testibus fit, cœteris excellet. (Menochius de Præsumptionibus, l. 1, q. 1.)

discovered; but who can say, how many instances have occurred, where the mistake has never been discovered?

It has often happened, that the real murderer has confessed the fact for which the innocent man has suffered; but, as real murderers do not always confess when innocent men suffer, it is impossible to say to what length this dangerous doctrine may have been carried.

Thirdly. I have further to observe, that this principle is new to the practice of the English law.

That great collection of criminal cases, which bears the name of the State Trials, contains a great fund of criminal knowledge.

The opinions of the judges, however, as expressed in state prosecutions, are not always to be regarded as law, until we reach the period of the revolution.

New enactments of the legislature have changed some part of the law, and the improving experience of time has altered others. The first notice to be found of this principle, in sound and wholesome times, is on the trial of Miss Blandy, for poisoning her father,—before Mr. Baron LEGGE, in 1752.

The judge, in summing up the evidence to the jury, declares that circumstances are more convincing and satisfactory than any other kind of evidence; because "*facts*," he says, "*cannot lie.*"*

That facts cannot lie, is sound logic, no doubt. Men only lie. But as we only know facts through the medium of witnesses, the truth of the fact depends always upon the truth of the witness; so that, although he furnishes us with a thousand facts, it is of no consequence, if he himself is unsound.

The next occasion on which this doctrine appears, is on the celebrated trial of Captain Donnellan, in 1781, before Mr. Justice BULLER, in the passage already quoted. But he has altered the position a little, by shifting the criterion from facts

* State Trials, v. 10, p. 32.

to circumstances. Facts, before, were the standard of truth; circumstances are now made to be so. For circumstances cannot lie. But what else are circumstances but facts, or *minor* facts; and I must take the liberty to say, that circumstances are still more liable to deceive, or to lead to deception, than even facts. A fact being more an object of sight, is easier apprehended by the senses than a circumstance; which, from its triviality, often escapes the attention altogether, is misapprehended, or assigned to a wrong cause.

The trial in question, will afford a most unparalleled illustration of the truth of this observation; it will show the fallibility of circumstances, and the very opposite conclusions which different men will draw from the same appearances.

I shall here give the general shape of the case—

> If shape it might be called, which shape had none,
> Or substance might be called, which shadow seemed.

Sir Theodosius Boughton, a young man of a delicate constitution, had sent to a country apothecary's shop for a draught of medicine. Different vials appear to have been in his chamber, at the time he took the draught; which was intended to be a composition of rhubarb, jalap, and lavender water.

He was suddenly seized with convulsions in his stomach, and foaming at the mouth; and expired before he could give any explanation. On rinsing one of the vials, the sediment gave the effluvia of laurel water, which is known to be a strong poison. Convulsions, foaming at the mouth, and sudden death, are the natural effects of that liquid.

But every man who dies in that way, is not, therefore, poisoned. The apoplexy will produce the same effects and appearances: of which disease, the father of the young man was known to have died. No evidence whatever was produced as to the existence of the laurel water.

Captain Donnellan, the brother-in-law of Sir Theodosius,

was living in his house at the time of the accident. He was the next heir to the estate, and, accordingly, the person who had the most immediate interest in his death. He certainly betrayed some uneasiness on the event, and appearances indicated that he was afraid of being suspected as the author of the mischief. But, if it was natural that he should be suspected, if the *cui bono* points out the actor of a nefarious deed, it was not unnatural that he should find himself placed in circumstances of peculiar delicacy, and manifest embarrassment and confusion in his conduct.

Captain Donnellan was brought to trial, on a charge of poisoning Sir Theodosius Boughton.

The leading point in every case of this sort, is—did the deceased die of poison? For, if he did not, there is an end of the whole. Where there was no poison, there was no poisoner.

But this was altogether a question to be decided by the opinion of medical men. From what then did they form their opinion? From any of those broad marks, respecting which all men judge alike. No; there was nothing of the kind to guide their judgment. The whole cause turned on circumstances, from first to last. Presumptions were formed on conjectures; and conjectures supposed from circumstances never proved. Four physicians inspected the body, on dissection, the eleventh day after the death. They gave their opinion to the jury, and described the circumstances on which that opinion was founded; those four said, they believed him to have died of poison.

The circumstances on which they had given their opinion, were stated, at the trial, to Doctor John Hunter, the most eminent physician of the age. He declared he could not discover, in any of those circumstances, nor in all of them united, any sign of the deceased having died from poison, nor any symptoms beyond those incident to a man dying suddenly.

Q. from the court to Mr. Hunter. Then, in your judgment, upon the appearance the gentlemen have described, no inference can be drawn from thence that Sir Theodosius

Boughton died of poison?—*A.* Certainly not: it does not give the least suspicion.

In questions of science, and above all, in those of medical science, the faith to be reposed in any opinion, will be regulated by the professional eminence of the person giving it. One man's sight being generally as good as that of another, as to a mere matter of fact; as whether he saw, or did not see such a thing, the learned and the ignorant are upon a par, and one witness to a fact is just as good as another. But the case is very different as to a matter of science; for one man's judgment will outweigh that of many. Upon a point of law or equity, we would not put the opinion of a country attorney, or of four country attorneys, against that of a chief justice, Doctor John Hunter stood, at that time, at the very head of his profession; his opinion gave the law to that profession, both in England and in every country in Europe. Had the profession been to estimate his opinion, and not the jury, a very different verdict would have been given. The case referred peculiarly to to Doctor Hunter's line of study,—that of dissection, and the appearances incident to a body on sudden and convulsive death. He pronounced, that the dissection had been irregularly made, and in a way not to afford the true criterion to judge by. And, where the process is irregular, when the experiment is defective, the conclusion must always be vague and doubtful.

The gentlemen composing the jury did not perhaps know the eminence of Mr. Hunter's character; nor, consequently, the weight due to his opinion. But the judge, on the bench, no doubt knew this; and in balancing the evidence, and in summing up, it was clearly his duty to have stated the great weight to be attached to Mr. Hunter's observations. He stated nothing of all this; but took them numerically, "four medical men to one."

Thus, from an irregular dissection, a positive conclusion was admitted.

It is a rule of law, and above all in cases of life and death, that the want of any one circumstance will prevent the effect of the whole. Thus, if the dissection were irregular, the opinion formed in reference to that dissection was a mere nothing. As well may you suppose that proposition itself to be true, which you wish to prove, as that other, whereby you hope to prove it.

Post hoc; ergo propter hoc—a species of argument which often leads to fallacy.

Because the fact immediately followed; therefore it was occasioned by that which it followed. He died immediately after taking the medicine; therefore, he was killed by the medicine.

The present question is, was the process on the trial according to law? Was the conclusion arrived at by regular and legal forms? The grounds on which the legal inference is to be drawn, must always of themselves be clear and certain; there is no presumption upon a presumption; there is no inference from a fact not known.

When the judgment of the law is passed in reference to a certain thing, the existence of that thing should be first clearly made to appear.

The fact of poisoning ought to have been established beyond a shadow of doubt, before any person was convicted as the poisoner.

But the jury, it will be said, were satisfied on this point. Had the evidence been duly summed up by the judge; had they been told, as they ought to have been, that in experimental philosophy, such as tracing the effects of a particular poison, in tracing the causes, so many and so complicated that lead to death, if the experiment is defective, if the process is vitiated in one instance, the result is also vitiated and defective. Every practitioner in philosophy is sensible and aware of this truth; and wherever he finds that he has erred in his experiment, he sets the case aside, as affording no satisfactory result, and renews his process in another subject.

But, unfortunately, it is a matter of pride, in some men,

to be always certain in their opinion, and to appear beyond the influence of doubt. Very different was the practice of that modest and eminent man who gave his evidence on this trial: he was accustomed to the fallaciousness of appearances, —to the danger of hasty inferences from imperfect proofs, and refused to give his assent to an opinion, without facts being first produced to support it. "If I knew," said Mr. Hunter, "that the draught was poison, I should say, most probably, that the symptoms arose from that; but when I don't know that that draught was poison, when I consider that a number of other things might occasion his death, I cannot answer positively to it."

During the whole course of this celebrated trial, there was not a single fact established by evidence, except the death, and convulsive appearances at the moment. These appearances, Mr. Hunter declared, offered no suspicion whatever of poison, and were generally incident to sudden death, in what might be called a state of health; not only there was no fact proved, but there was not one single circumstance proved. One circumstance was supposed from another, equally suppositious, and from two fictions united a third was produced. The existence of the laurel water was thus made out: the sediment found in the vial, from which the unfortunate young man had drunk, was supposed to smell like bitter almonds; for, as the smell of laurel water was not then known to Lady Boughton, she could not trace the resemblance further; bitter almonds were supposed to smell like laurel water.

It is here to be observed, that the smell attached to the vial was momentary, for it was washed out almost immediately, and could not be twice experienced. But what so uncertain as the sense of smell? Of all the human senses, it is the most uncertain, the most variable, and fallacious. It is often different to different men, and different in the same person, at one hour, from what it is at the next; a cold, a slight indisposition, the state of the stomach, a sudden exposure to the air, will extenuate or destroy this impression.

But this train of proof was altogether at variance with principles. In law, as already observed, the arguments should be drawn from one reality to another; but here, the argument turned upon the breath, the smell of a woman, distracted at the moment, with the loss of her son, and ready to ascribe that evil to the first thing that came in her way.

All proof must begin at a fixed point. The law never admits of an inference from an inference. Two imperfect things cannot make one perfect. That which is weak, may be made stronger; but that which has no substance, cannot be corroborated. The question is never what a thing is like; but the witness must swear to his belief, as to what it is. A simile is no argument. Upon the principle, that comparison of hands is no evidence, in a criminal trial, comparison of smells must be held to be equally defective. Besides, there are a variety of articles that resemble bitter almonds in the smell, and many of these altogether innoxious.

In circumstantial evidence, the circumstance and the presumption are too often confounded; as they seem to have been throughout this trial. The circumstance is always a fact; the presumption is the inference drawn from that fact. It is hence called presumptive proof; because it proceeds merely on presumption or opinion. But the circumstance itself is never to be presumed, but must be substantively proved. An argument ought to consist in something that is itself admitted; for who can prove one doubtful thing by another. If it was not laurel water, that Sir Theodosius drank, the proof fails as to the effect; and, certainly, some of the usual proofs, some of the common *indicia* or marks of things, should have been established. Where did the prisoner procure it? From whom did he obtain it? Where, and what time,—and by whom, or how did he administer it?* Nothing of this kind was proved.

The whole proof, as to laurel water, rested upon the com-

* Venenum arguis: ubi emi? a quo? quanti? per quem dedi? quo conscio? Quintilian, l. 5, c. 8, s. 37

parison of the smell. Question to Doctor Parsons, "You ground your opinion upon the description of its smell by Lady Boughton?" Answer. "Yes, we can ground our opinion upon nothing else but that, and the subsequent effects."

But the judgment of the cause from its effects, Mr. Hunter has already shown to be equally conjectural as that formed from its resemblance in smell.

The proof proceeds. He was supposed to be poisoned, because it was believed to be laurel water; and it was believed to be laurel water, because he was supposed to be poisoned. We will not say that both these suppositions might not have been true; yet still they were but conjectures, unsupported by any proof, and formed against all the rules of law.

But the accused, it is said, furnished the proof against himself, by his own distrust of his innocence. He no doubt betrayed great apprehensions of being charged with the murder; but are innocent men never afraid of being thought guilty?

We readily recognize all the general truisms, and commonplace observations, as to the confidence of innocence, and the consciousness of guilt; but, we find, from history, that innocence loses its confidence, when oppressed with prejudice; and that men have been convicted of crimes, which they never committed, from the very means which they have taken to clear themselves.

"An uncle who had the bringing up of his niece, to whom he was heir at law, correcting her for some offense, she was heard to say, 'Good uncle, do not kill me;' after which time she could not be found; whereupon the uncle was committed upon suspicion of murder, and admonished, by the justices of the assize, to find out the child by the next assizes; against which time he could not find her, but brought another child, as like her in years and person as he could find, and apparelled her like the true child; but on examination she was found not to be the true child. Upon these presumptions (which were considered to be as strong as facts that appear in the broad face of day), he was found guilty and executed;

but the truth was, the child, being beaten, ran away, and was received by a stranger; and afterwards, when she came of age to have her land, came and demanded it, and was directly proved to be the true child.*

The above case was referred to by Lord MANSFIELD, in his speech in the Douglass cause, as an illustration that forgery, and falsehood itself, has been sometimes used to defend even an innocent cause. "It was no uncommon thing," he observed, "for a man to defend a good cause by foul means, or false pretenses."

Captain Donnellan was liable to suspicion, and to great suspicion, on the general relations of the subject, independent of particular circumstances, and would have been suspected by all the world, had he been never so innocent.

In the first place, it was a well-known fact, that he had been obliged either to quit the army (to which he originally belonged), or had been cashiered by the sentence of a court-martial.

Secondly, he was of all other men the person who was to have gained by the death of Sir Theodosius Boughton; to whose estate and property he succeeded as his brother-in-law. No other human being had an interest in the case. Such is the disposition in human nature (founded perhaps on a too just knowledge of our feelings and principles of action), that first suspicion always points to the person who is to gain by it, as the author of any mischief of which the real perpetrator is not known. The *cui bono* was not invented by Cassius Severus, to whom it is ascribed,—but every man is alike the *rock of the accused,* in this respect.

If, therefore, it was natural, on general grounds, that Mr. Donnellan should be so suspected, it was also natural for him to be sensible that he would be so, and consequently, to be alarmed, distracted, and uneasy.

But it will be said, that, granting all this, he displayed

* Hale's Pleas of the Crown, v. 2, p. 290.

more uneasiness than was even natural to one in his situation. It is a delicate thing to answer this question,—it is a nice thing to fix the standard of human feelings,—and to say what degree of perturbation a man, already branded with guilt and conviction, shall feel when placed under circumstances which make him to be suspected of a capital crime.

Lawyers, and those accustomed to see and advise with persons in that unfortunate predicament, only can tell the terrible apprehensions that every man feels at the idea of being a second time brought to a public trial; it is altogether a new view of human nature, and we seldom estimate, rightly, feelings which we have never experienced, nor expect to experience in our own persons, nor have witnessed in that of other persons;—

> " To thee no reason,—
> " Who good has only known, and evil has not proved."

They who have been accustomed to carry on criminal prosecutions, must be fully aware of the influence which a former trial and conviction is calculated to have on almost any accusation; but in no case can that influence be greater than where the trial turns on presumptive proof. For here it is often the feelings, the prejudices, and opinion of the the jury, that supply the want of evidence.

Suspicion is to be distinguished from proof,—a thousand suspicions do not form one proof. We understand, in common language, by the term suspicion, the imagining of something ill, without proof. It may, therefore, form a proper ground of accusation, but never of conviction: it seems to arise from the general semblance of things, and often from the morals of the individual, rather than from any distinct act. Thus, in the civil law, a guardian is regarded as suspected, whose morals render him so.

A suspicion is one thing, and a necessary inference another: a suspicion is an impression on another man's mind, —an inference is made from the fact itself.

There certainly was no overt act proved against the prisoner during the whole course of this trial; it was not proved that he gave the poison, or saw it given, or had such in his possession. Many things, no doubt, in his demeanor and conversation, gave strong suspicions against him; but, if the civil law positively forbids a man being condemned on suspicion, can that be justified by ours?

"The wisdom and goodness of our law appears in nothing more remarkably, than in the perspicuity, certainty, and clearness of the evidence it requires to fix a crime upon any man, whereby his life, his liberty, or his property can be concerned: herein we glory and pride ourselves, and are justly the envy of all our neighbor nations. Our law, in such cases, requires evidence so clear and convincing, that every bystander, the instant he hears it, must be fully satisfied of the truth and certainty of it. It admits of no surmises, innuendoes, forced consequences, or harsh constructions, nor anything else to be offered as evidence, but what is real and substantial, according to the rules of natural justice and equity."*

We have been the more full in our observations on this trial, because it has been so often quoted with a sort of triumph, as forming a model and illustration of the nature of circumstantial evidence. It is an illustration, indeed, of how little evidence one man has been convicted on; but it is an illustration of nothing else.

We can never bring ourselves to believe, that it is necessary to forfeit the life of a man on bare suspicion, on presumptions without proof, and on inferences unsupported by evidence.

A rule of conduct, to be good, must be so on general grounds, and in reference to the state of society in which we

* Lord Cowper's speech on the Bishop of Rochester's trial.

are placed; and, happily, the wholesome state of British morals does not require that men should be convicted on any evidence but that which is established by law, and warranted by sound reason.

The mischief of a nice conviction does not rest with the particular case; precedents are grounds of law by the English practice, and indeed the most general ground of our law of evidence.

We have, in more than one instance, witnessed the doctrine of circumstantial evidence being hastily applied by loose analogies and incidents, foreign to the intrinsic conditions of the subject. But we do not feel ourselves at liberty to hurt the tenderness due to living reputation, by recurrence to recent instances; we adopt the more agreeable duty of bearing testimony to the wise maxim of an eminent magistrate: "Nothing can be more dangerous or unjust, in matters of this nature," says Mr. Chief Justice HYDE, speaking of homicide, "than to establish material distinctions upon points which do not enter into the intrinsic merits of the case." (*East's Pleas of the Crown*, p. 241.)

The evidence of circumstances on every criminal trial, should be confined as much as possible to the actual commission of the fact.

The intention, indeed, must always precede the act, and is chiefly to be judged of by the antecedent circumstances. But then each of these circumstances should be regarded as a fact to be proved and established by evidence; and, unless so established, ought never to form a ground of conviction. We must once more revert to the trial for illustration. On passing sentence, Mr. Justice BULLER conveyed the following opinion as to the motives:—"Probably the greatness of his fortune caused the greatness of your offense; and I am fully satisfied, on the evidence given against you, that avarice was your motive, and hypocrisy served you with the means."

But where or how was this proved by evidence on the trial? The speech of a judge is to be taken out of the evidence adduced on the trial;—if it is not so limited, it may be difficult to fix its bounds.

In a criminal trial, and more especially in the trial for a capital offense, everything is supposed to be governed by fixed and known rules. There is here no room for the discretion of a judge; the proof by which the prisoner is to be tried is as fixed as the law which condemns the crime; at least, the principles of that proof are to be stated by the judge to the jury, as known and received maxims of reason, handed down by a long train of precedents, or fixed by statutory enactment. "Whatever the rules in Westminister Hall are, it is not therefore reason because it is a rule; but because it is reason, and reason approved of by long experience, therefore it is a rule." (*State Trials*, vol. 4, p. 291.) The opinion of Mr. Justice BULLER might have been very just, but if it was not regularly formed, it was extra-judicial and of dangerous example.

It is an observation warranted by the history of our criminal law, that all the instances by which innocent men have lost their lives, have arisen from precedents against guilty men;* but laws were meant to protect the innocent, as well as to punish the guilty.

The following observation, by Lord BACON, suggests the caution with which men should give their assent to any proposition founded on a mere similarity of circumstances:—"The mind," he observes, "has this property,—that it readily supposes a greater order and conformity in things than it finds; and although many things in nature are singular, and extremely dissimilar, yet the mind is still imagining parallel correspondence and relations betwixt them which have no existence.

"Nor does this folly," he adds, "prevail only in abstract tenets, but also in simple notions." (*Novum organum, s.* 2. *aphorim* 45.)

* Omnia mala exampla, ex bonis initiis orta sun.

Every one may prove the justice of these remarks, by his reflections on what he sees every day occurring in common life.

Weak men are always the first to assent and to admit of loose analogies, imperfect resemblances, and inferences without proof,—whilst men of stronger minds, and more reflection, look out for distinctions; they search for discriminations in subjects nearly similar, and are slow in yielding their assent to first impressions. Judgment consists in distinguishing things which are nearly alike, without exactly being so.

In the general prejudice, which at present prevails for circumstantial evidence, the mind, I am afraid, is rather disposed to look out for analogies and resemblances, than for discrimination.

In almost every trial, it is the interest of the accuser to accumulate his proofs, whilst the safety of the prisoner consists in considering these, separate and apart; this practice, therefore, has a tendency rather to convict than to acquit.

We should lament to advance any thing that might tend to weaken the facility of detecting crimes; but that facility may be increased by establishing certain rules for the determination of proof.

Without presuming to state a body of general rules, we may be allowed to show where some obvious principles have been violated. All instruction proceeds safest by negatives and exclusives to what is positive and affirmative. And it was this principle which led us to dwell so particularly on the above case. We conceive one great error has arisen from the popular saying, that circumstances cannot lie; from the idea that circumstantial evidence is equivalent to direct proof.

And, perhaps, from the vanity of forming resemblances, where (if that passion in the judicial character is ever allowable), the vanity should rather be in perceiving distinctions.

Nothing is more dangerous in the mouth of a judge, than popular brocards, barren generalities, and loose unsettled maxims, which carry away the attention of the jury from the intrinsic evidence of the case itself, and prevent the free exercise of their own understandings. It is not every jury-man that can understand a general theory, but every man of sense can compare what he hears at the trial, with similar circumstances, as falling under his own experience, and so estimate for himself the credibility of the evidence.

I deprecate an argumentative judge, reasoning a jury into a belief of guilt or innocence, rather than leaving them to judge from their own feelings; from those feelings which God and nature have bestowed on them, as the safeguard of innocence, and the true measure of human conduct.

The following observation, in the charge so often alluded to, deserves particular remark:—"It is not within the reach and compass of human abilities to invent a train of circumstances which shall be so connected together as to amount to a proof, without affording opportunities of contradicting a great part, if not all, of these circumstances."

This is one of those general sayings which, coming from high authority, is allowed to pass without examination, and, from being often repeated, no one thinks to doubt of its truth. No other remark, however, was ever more refuted by experience. If the observation was just, we should find it illustrated by practice; but we know that there are infinitely more instances of mistaken convictions on circumstantial evidence, than by any other species of proof whatever. "Reducing general words to particular facts, clears the sophistry of them."*

I beg here to dwell, a little more minutely, on the hardship of requiring a prisoner to controvert a train of circumstantial evidence. For, how can a prisoner, altogether innocent of the charge, controvert circumstances, or an account of events, with which he is unacquainted. A man, charged with the commission of a crime, at a period long an-

* Remarks on College's trial, by Sir J. Hawles. State Trials, vol. 3, p. 621.

terior to the trial, if innocent, and at a distance from the place, at the time of its occurrence, can only establish his innocence by one of two methods:—first, by showing a contradiction in the circumstances of the proof itself; or, secondly, by establishing an *alibi*,—that is, by showing that he was at a different place at the time.* In regard to the first mode of refuting the charge: if he is ignorant of the facts, if he is unaccustomed to the nature of legal argument, he may not easily confute the chain of circumstances. A premeditated story is always so made up as to bear the appearance of consistency. Men will believe a probable falsehood rather than a singular truth; and, in regard to the proof of an *alibi*, if the prisoner does not happen to recollect the day, or cannot, perhaps, recall to mind where he chanced to be on that day, he is left without a defense. The proof of a negative is always difficult, often impossible.

But what is the situation of a person charged with a capital crime? Suspicions of this sort generally fall upon the needy and unfortunate. He is brought from a jail, where he has been perhaps long confined, distracted and agitated with his situation; he has none to assist him or suggest to him what course to pursue; and no counsel is allowed to plead for him, and assert his innocency of the facts charged. A long train of circumstances are offered by the witnesses, of the whole of which he is ignorant, and, therefore, unprepared to ask the necessary questions, or to point out to the jury the incongruity of the story advanced:—his very attempt to do so, unsuccessfully (that is to say, if he makes observations on the evidence, which are not explanatory or correct), will be held an argument of his guilt. But the facts have been sworn to, and his personal appearance is perhaps against him; and his character,—it may be, suffering under prejudice. If a weak magistrate happens to sit on the bench (and weak men

* The character of the witnesses is, no doubt, always a matter of the most important consideration.

sometimes find their way to the bench, as well as to other places); if the judge is infirm, or his attention exhausted by the fatigue of a long trial; and if, in summing up, he loses sight of the chain of incidents, assumes a fact as established before it is so,—endeavors to prove facts by other facts, which are not proved themselves,—forgets the attention which is due to the character of the witnesses, and has allowed the counsel for the prosecution, in his opening speech, to prejudice and inflame the minds of the jury!—

It were superfluous to ask what the result of such a trial must naturally be. We hope, and believe, that such a concurrence of incidents, hostile to justice, is very uncommon.

But to return to the proposition in the charge: can it ever be admitted that the number of circumstances alleged against a prisoner, facilitates the refutation? Surely the difficulty of defense is increased by the multiplicity of proof that it has to contend with! The attention is distracted; and the very embarrassment incident to the occasion, is alone sufficient to bereave any common man of his faculties.

The civil law has foreseen the embarrassments, which a prisoner must always be under, from a variety of witnesses being produced against him; and has, therefore, left it to the discretion of the judge to moderate their number. It might as well be said, that a prisoner has an advantage in the multiplicity of witnesses opposed to him, because if false he can always refute some of them.

But, if you break the chain of circumstances, it will be said, in one link, the whole structure falls to the ground. This, no doubt, ought to be the consequence. But is the fact so? Does experience warrant the observation? Are we to suppose that all those who have been irregularly convicted, made no defense, and broke no part of the chain? They must naturally have offered something to the consideration of the jury. Yet still, we see, that the general effect of the whole, the multiplicity of the circumstances, pointing against the prisoner, has been thought sufficient to warrant conviction.

It happens, not unfrequently, that a prisoner is not apprized of the evidence intended to be produced against him. If the case is altogether false on the part of the prosecution, the difficulty of defense is increased. For a man can only refute a false story, by being acquainted with some part of it. The true case must always be opposed to the false one. Thus, in the case of two men who were tried some few years ago, for the murder of Mr. Steele, on Hounslow Heath, a long detail of the circumstances attending the occasion, was given in evidence against them. But if they were not, as they asserted, present on the occasion, and knew nothing of either Mr. Steele or the murder, how was it possible for them to refute or disprove the circumstances?

The accusation was not brought until some years after the murder. They could not bring to recollection where they were on that day, and so failed in establishing an alibi.

A different man has been since brought to trial for that very murder. It is true that the judges did not allow the evidence to be entered upon, because they thought that it was insufficient on the statement of the counsel in his opening speech.

It should be always kept in mind, that circumstantial evidence is merely supplemental; and is only resorted to from the want of original and direct proof. And it never can be said that what is secondary, is equal to that which is original, —the thing substituted equal to that which it is meant to supply.

And this distinction seems fully recognized by Lord Chief Baron Gilbert. "When the fact itself cannot be proved, that which comes nearest to the proof of the fact, is the proof of the circumstances that necessarily and usually attend such facts, and called presumptions; and not proof, for they stand instead of the proofs of the fact till the contrary be proved." (*Gilbert's Law of Evidence*, vol. 1, p. 142.)

A regard to the peace and good order of society, certainly requires that crimes shall be liable to be proved by circumstantial evidence. But a regard to the well being of society likewise demands, that the mode of proof should be regulated by some fixed rules. If the nature of the thing admits of but few rules, for that very reason, those few should be the more distinctly observed. This principle is excellently illustrated by the deep Gravina, who somewhere observes (for the book is not at hand for reference), that as the military state admits of but few laws, those few should be the more distinctly observed, as they could only have been introduced into an army or camp from a strong sense of their necessity.

Legal proceedings would be vague and uncertain, judges would become arbitrary, and innocence would be exposed to the resentment of witnesses, if some general and fixed rules were not observed for the discovery of truth.

Of these the following are perhaps the chief:—

1. *The actual commission of the crime itself* (*the corpus delicti*) *shall be clearly established.*

2. *Each circumstance shall be distinctly proved.*

3. *The circumstance relied on, shall be such as is necessary or usually incident to the fact charged.*

4. *When the number of circumstances depend on the testimony of one witness, that number shall not increase the strength of the proof.* For, as the whole depends on the veracity of the witness, when that fails the whole fails.

5. *Direct evidence shall not be held refuted from being opposed to circumstances incongruous with that evidence.* Because a certain degree of incongruity is incident to every man's conduct.

6. *The judge, in summing up, shall assume no fact or circumstance as proved; but shall state the whole hypothetically and conditionally; leaving it entirely to the jury, to determine how far the case is made out to their satisfaction.*

7. *The difficulty of proving the negative shall in all cases be allowed due weight.* But the silence of the prisoner as to

facts, which, if innocent, he might have explained, shall be held an argument against him. This, of course, proceeds upon the supposition, that he stood fully apprized, before his trial, of all that was intended to be produced.

8. *The counsel for the prisoner shall be allowed to object freely to the production of any evidence, as not proper to go to the jury, or as not being of legal credence.* On Captain Donnellan's trial, the counsel do not appear to have always availed themselves of this privilege.

The liberty of objecting to any piece of evidence, ought, on every occasion, to be strenuously exerted; as supplying, in a great measure, the right of making the defense.

9. *The jury shall be as fully convinced of the guilt of the prisoner, from the combination of the circumstances, as if direct proof had been brought.*

It should always be considered, whether the connection betwixt the circumstances and the crime is necessary, or only casual and contingent; and whether, therefore, the circumstances necessarily involve the guilt of the prisoner, or only probably so; whether these circumstances might not all exist, and yet the accused be innocent.

It seems desirable, that some inchoate act, approaching to the crime, should be proved on the prisoner; and that he should not be convicted on general appearances,—such as from being found in a certain situation. The improper conviction seem chiefly to have been owing to a neglect of this rule. Strong appearances, but without any act proved against the prisoner, have too often turned out unfounded.

It is sometimes said, in summing up by the judge, that the evidence is the best that the nature of the case can be supposed to afford; but this, certainly, is no reason for the jury being satisfied with it. In the first place, the nature of the case is only to be known by the evidence. The case of an innocent man must always be of a nature to afford very little evidence; but the jury, let the case be what it will, must be distinctly persuaded of the guilt of the prisoner, before they return such a verdict. Agreeably to the common law, where the facts have gone regularly before a jury, and there is no misdirection from the judge in summing up, the proof is complete. When the jury is satisfied, the law is satisfied. No principle can be at once more calculated to facilitate the detection of crimes, to ensure the safety of innocence, and to maintain the general peace of society.

10. *Where the body of the act is distinctly sworn to, a variation in the circumstances does not destroy the proof.* "If several independent witnesses, of fair character, should agree in all the parts of a story (in testifying, for instance, that a murder or a robbery was committed at a particular time, in a particular place, and by a certain individual), every court of justice in the world would admit the fact, notwithstanding the abstract possibility of the whole being false. Again, if several honest men should agree in saying that they saw the king of France beheaded, though they should disagree as to the figure of the guillotine, or the size of his executioner, as to the king's head being bound or loose, as to his being composed or agitated in ascending the scaffold, yet every court of justice in the world would think that such difference, respecting the circumstances of the fact, did not invalidate the evidence respecting the fact itself.

"When you speak of the whole of a story, you cannot mean every particular circumstance connected with the history, but not essential to it; you must mean the pith and marrow of a story; for it would be impossible to establish the truth of any fact (of Admirals Byng or Keppel, for example, having neglected or not neglected their duty), if a disagreement in the evidence of witnesses, in minute points, should be considered as annihilating the weight of the evidence in points of importance. In a word, the relation of a fact differs essentially from the demonstration of a theorem; if one step is left out, one link in the chain of ideas constituting a demonstration is omitted, the conclusion will be destroyed; but a fact may be established notwithstanding a disagreement of witnesses in certain trifling particulars of their evidence respecting it."*

The following rule is the converse of the preceding one:

11. *Where the leading fact or crime is only to be collected from circumstances, a material variation in these will defeat the effect of the whole.*

For, as each particular is to have an effect on the general conclusion, a variation in the circumstances may give a different color to the whole transaction.

A system of propositions is only true, because each of the propositions, of which it is composed, is true.

12. *There being no repugnance in the chain of circumstances, is a proof that a thing may be; not that it is: though there being a repugnance, is a proof that it cannot be.* Whatever does not involve a contradiction, is possible; whatever involves one, is impossible.

13. *The absence of the proof, naturally to be expected, is a strong argument against the existence of any fact alleged.* This applies particularly to cases where violence is charged.

"It is an undoubted truth" (Lord MANSFIELD observed in the Douglass cause), "that judges, in forming their opinion of events, and in deciding upon the truth or falsehood of controverted facts, must be guided by the rules of probability; and, as mathematical or absolute certainty is seldom to be attained in human affairs, reason and public utility require that judges, and all mankind, in forming their opinion of the truth of facts, should be regulated by the superior number of the probabilities on the one side or the other,

* Apology for the Bible, p. 344.

We shall search in vain our State Trials, for a happier illustration of the principle than the above, from the elegant pen of Doctor Watson. "Literary men," it has been observed, "have marked superiority over lawyears, whenever they assume their profession."

Quæ argumenta ad quem modum probandæ cuique rei sufficiant, nullo certo modo satis definiri potest.

Ex sententia animi tui te æstimare oportet, quid aut credas, aut parum probatum tibi opinaris (ff. lib. 22, tit. 5, s. 3).

whether the amount of these probabilities be expressed in words and arguments, or by figures and numbers."

Applied to the affairs of civil life in reference to which the observation was made, the proposition is excellent; but the rule does not hold in criminal cases. The impression on the mind of the jury, in a criminal case, must be, not that the prisoner is probably guilty, but that he really and absolutely is so;—where they doubt, they are to acquit.

It is often said, in respect to evidence of this sort, if you break the chain of circumstances, the whole falls to the ground. It is material, always, to be apprised of the meaning of terms, before we argue as to their effect. What is the import of the term? In what does this interruption consist? The Douglass cause turned entirely on circumstantial evidence; yet neither the speeches of the judges, nor the singularly acute letters of Mr. Stewart, on the subject of the trial, afford any solution of the term. The chain appears, on both sides of the question, repeatedly broken, and as often renewed; the want of the fact is supplied by argument, and the argument invalidated by the want of the fact, in endless prolixity.

We hazard an explanation of it with great diffidence:—the chain of circumstances is broken, whenever there is such a defect in the thread of the narrative as cannot be accounted for; or, such a contradiction in the statement, as is irreconcilable with probability.

We will not add to the number of the above rules, lest we might appear to aim at forming a technical system for the belief or disbelief of facts, independent of the free exercise of the understanding over the circumstances of the case.

We must never bind ourselves down to believe or disbelieve, on general grounds, abstracted from the condition of times, persons, motives, and all the variety of relations of which the particular case happens to consist. Irregular, capricious, and shifting as man is, in all his actions, we can never establish absolute grounds for judging of these.

FAMOUS CASES

OF

CIRCUMSTANTIAL EVIDENCE.

I.

THERE lived in Paris, more than a century ago, an old dame who kept a shop in a house not far distant from the Place St. Michel. She was reputed rich, and was supposed to keep her money in the house. Her only servant was a boy who had lived with her for several years; he slept in the house, but high up in the fourth story, or rather loft, which could only be reached by a staircase, such as was common in those days, outside the house wall, the old lady sleeping in a room on the ground floor at the back of the shop. It was the boy's duty to lock the shop door at night and retain possession of the key. One morning the neighbors found the shop door open much earlier than usual, and as there was no one to be seen in the shop, some of them, suspecting that all was not right, went in. There were no marks betokening a violent entry of the premises, but the old lady was discovered dead in her bed, having received many wounds, such wounds, to all appearance, having been inflicted with a knife; and a knife covered with blood was found lying in the middle of the shop floor. One hand of the corpse yet grasped a thick lock of hair, and in the other was a neck-handkerchief. It was proved beyond doubt that the knife and the neck-handkerchief belonged to the boy who had been so long her servant, and the lock of hair also matched his exactly. He was arrested, charged with the crime, and (probably under torture) confessed it, and suffered capital punishment as a murderer. He was innocent, notwithstanding. Not very long after his execution another boy, a servant in a neighboring wine-shop, being taken into custody for another offense, and seized with the pangs of remorse, confessed to the murder of the old dame. He had long been familiarly acquainted with the shop boy, who had suffered innocently, and had been in the habit of dressing his hair. He had managed by degrees to save up enough of the lad's hair from the comb he made use of to make into a tolerably stout lock, and this he had put into the hand of the dead woman. He had stolen one of the boy's neck-handkerchiefs, and also his knife, and by taking an impression in wax of the key, had been able to construct another by which to gain entrance to the shop. At the first glance, the evidence in this case seems at once clear, natural and spontaneous; but the very completeness of the evidentiary facts ought to have aroused suspicion; and there is no doubt that had a rigid investigation been set on foot, the innocence of the accused would have been established.

II.

A case of fabricated evidence of a sufficiently remarkable kind occurred near Hull, in the year 1742. A gentleman traveling to that place was stopped late in the evening, about seven miles from the town, by a masked highwayman, who robbed him of a purse containing twenty guineas. The highwayman galloped off by a side road, and the traveler, in no way injured, save in purse, continued his journey. It was now growing late, and, being excited and alarmed by what had happened, he naturally looked out for a place of shelter, and, instead of riding on to Hull, stopped at the first inn he came to, which was the "Bell Inn," kept by Mr. James Brunell. He went into the kitchen to give directions for his supper, and there he related to several persons the fact of his having been robbed, to which he added the further information, that when he traveled he always gave his gold a peculiar mark, and that every guinea in the purse taken from him was thus marked. He hoped, therefore, that the robber would yet be detected. Supper being ready, he withdrew. The gentleman had not long finished his supper, when Mr. Brunell came into the parlor where he was, and, after the usual inquiries of landlords as to the desires of the guest, observed, "Sir, I understand you have been robbed in this neighborhood this evening?" "Yes," said the traveler, "I have." "And your money was marked?" continued the landlord. "It was so," was the reply. "A circumstance has arisen," resumed Mr. Brunell, "which leads me to think I can point out the robber. Pray, at what time in the evening were you stopped." "It was just setting in to be dark," replied the traveler. "The time confirms my suspicions," said the landlord; and he then informed the gentleman that he had a waiter, one John Jennings, who had of late been so very full of money, and so very extravagant, that he (the landlord) had been surprised at it, and had determined to part with him, his conduct being every way suspicious; that long before dark that day, he had sent out Jennings to change a guinea for him; that the man had only come back since the arrival of the traveler, saying he could not get change; and that, seeing Jennings to be in liquor, he had sent him off to bed, determined to discharge him in the morning. Mr. Brunell continued to say, that when the guinea was brought back to him, it struck him that it was not the same he had sent out for change, there being on the returned one a mark which he was very sure was not upon the other; but he should probably have thought no more of the matter, Jennings having frequently had gold in his pocket of late, had not the people in the kitchen told him what the traveler had related respecting the robbery, and the circumstance of the guineas being marked. He (Mr. Brunell) had not been present when this relation was made, and, unluckily, before he heard of it from the people in the kitchen, he had paid away the guinea to a man who lived at some distance, and who had now gone home. "The circumstance, however," said the landlord, in conclusion, "struck me so very strongly, that I could not refrain, as an honest man, from coming and giving you information of it."

Mr. Brunell was duly thanked for his disclosure. There appeared from it the strongest reasons for suspecting Jennings; and if, on searching him, any others of the marked guineas should be found, and the gentleman could identify them, there would then remain no doubt in the matter. It was now agreed to go up to his room. Jennings was fast asleep; his pockets were searched, and from one of them was drawn forth a purse containing exactly nineteen guineas. Suspicion now became certainty; for the traveler declared the purse and guineas to be identically those of which he had been robbed. Assistance was called; Jennings was awakened, dragged out of bed, and charged with the robbery. He denied it firmly; but the circumstances against him were too strong, and he was not believed. He was secured that night, and next day was taken before a justice of the peace. The gentleman and Mr. Brunell deposed to the facts upon oath; and Jennings, having no proofs, nothing but mere assertions of innocence, which could not be credited, was committed to take his trial at the next assizes.

So strong seemed the case against him, that most of the man's friends advised him to plead guilty, and throw himself on the mercy of the court. This advice he rejected, and when arraigned, pleaded not guilty. The prosecutor swore to the fact of the robbery; though, as it took place in the dusk, and the highwayman wore a mask, he could not swear to the person of the prisoner, but thought him of the same stature nearly as the man who robbed him. To the purse and guineas, when they were produced in court, he swore—as to the purse, positively, and as to the marked guineas, to the best of his belief; and he testified to their having been taken from the pocket of the prisoner.

The prisoner's master, Mr. Brunell, deposed as to the sending of Jennings for the change of a guinea, and to the waiter's having brought him back a marked one instead of the one he had given him unmarked. He also gave evidence as to the discovery of the purse and guineas on the prisoner. To consummate the proof, the man to whom Mr. Brunell had paid the guinea, as mentioned, came forward and produced the coin, testifying at the same time, that he had received it on the evening of the robbery, from the prisoner's master, in payment of a debt; and the prosecutor, on comparing it with the other nineteen, swore to its being, to the best of his belief, one of the twenty marked coins taken from him by the highwayman, and of which the other nineteen were found on Jennings.

The judge summed up the evidence, pointing out all the concurring circumstances against the prisoner; and the jury, convinced by this strong accumulation of testimony, without going out of court, brought in a verdict of guilty. Jennings was executed some time afterwards, at Hull, repeatedly declaring his innocence up to the moment of his execution.

Within a twelvemonth afterwards, Brunell, the master of Jennings, was himself taken up for a robbery committed on a guest in his house, and the fact being proved on trial, he was convicted and ordered for execution. The approach of death brought on repentance and confession. Brunell not only acknowledged he had been guilty of many highway robberies, but owned that he had committed the very one for which Jennings suffered. The account which he gave was, that after robbing the traveler, he had reached home before him by swifter riding, and by a nearer way. That he found a man at home waiting for him, to whom he owed a little bill, and to whom, not having enough of other money in his pocket, he gave away one of the guineas which he had just obtained by robbery. Presently came in the robbed gentleman, who, whilst Brunell, not knowing of his arrival, was in the stable, told his tale, as before related, in the kitchen. The gentleman had scarcely left the kitchen before Brunell entered it, and there, to his consternation, heard of the facts, and of the guineas being marked. He became dreadfully alarmed. The guinea which he had paid away he dared not ask back again; and as the affair of the robbery, as well as the circumstance of the marked guineas, would soon become publicly known, he saw nothing before him but detection, disgrace, and death. In this dilemma, the thought of accusing and sacrificing poor Jennings occurred to him. The state of intoxication in which Jennings was, gave him an opportunity of concealing the purse of money in the waiter's pocket. The rest the reader knows.

III.

James Harris kept a public house within eighteen miles of York, having in his service a man named Morgan, who, to his other occupations, added that of gardener. It happened that one Grey, a blacksmith, journeying on foot to Edinburgh, supped and slept at this public house. Next morning Morgan deposed before a magistrate, that his master strangled Grey in his bed—that he actually saw him commit the murder—that he in vain endeavored to prevent it, his master insisting that the man was in a fit, and that he was merely endeavoring to assist him. Morgan further swore, that, affecting to believe this, he left the room; but after retiring, looked through the keyhole, and saw the murderer rifling the pockets of the deceased. Harris, as well he might, vehemently denied the accusation, and, haplessly for himself, threatened a prosecution for perjury. As no mark of violence was visible on the body, Harris was on the point of being discharged, when the maid-servant demanded to be heard. She swore that from a wash house window, as she was descending the stairs, she saw her master take some gold from his pocket, and having carefully wrapped it up, bury it under a tree in the garden, the position of which she indicated. Upon this, Harris turned pale, and the earth under the tree having been searched by a constable, thirty pounds in gold was found wrapped up in a paper. Harris then admitted that he had buried the money for security's sake, but answered in so confused and hesitating manner, that he was committed. He was tried at York for the murder. The man, the maid, the constable, and the magistrate, were all examined, and no suspicion attaching to their testimony, a verdict of guilty was at once pronounced. He died protesting his innocence, and ere long his innocence became manifest to all men. The real facts were as follows. In a quarrel between Harris and his servant, Morgan received a blow, and vowed revenge. Soon afterwards, Grey's arrival furnished the opportunity. The part which the servant maid played in the business is explained by the fact that she and the gardener were sweethearts. Seeing her master one day apparently hiding something under a tree, she apprised Morgan, who, on digging, found five guineas concealed there. On this, they agreed to purloin the hoard, when it should amount to a sum sufficient to enable them to set up in business. But

Harris's threat of a prosecution for perjury so terrified the girl, that she resolved to save her lover by the sacrifice both of the money and of her master's life. A subsequent quarrel, the not unusual consequence of guilt like theirs, betrayed the truth. They died of jail fever, on the day previous to that appointed for their trial. It was afterwards ascertained that Grey had had two apoplectic fits, and had never been in possession of five pounds at a time in his life.

In this melancholy case, it will be observed that the victim of circumstantial evidence himself unconsciously prepared the principal fact which told against him.

IV.

The most striking case of circumstantial evidence, in which the testimony against the accused was altogether fabricated by the accuser, is one taken from the Danish records, and which, from its impressiveness, has been made the subject of remark by both Danish and German writers. The unhappy fate of the clergyman, Sören Qvist, is familiar to his countrymen, though many generations have passed away since the events which are about to be related.

Sören was the pastor of the little village of Veilby, situated a few miles from Grenaee, in the Jutland peninsula. He was a man of excellent moral character, generous, hospitable, and diligent in the performance of his sacred duties ; but he was also a man of constitutionally violent temper, which he lacked the ability to restrain, and was consequently subject at times to fierce outbreaks of wrath, which were a scourge to his household when they occurred, and a humiliation to himself. Like most Danish clergymen of that day, he was a tiller of the soil, as well as a preacher of the word; and from the produce of his tithes, and the cultivation of his farm, realized a comfortable competence. He was a widower with two children—a daughter who kept house for him, and a son holding an officer's commission in the army. At Ingvorstrup, a village not far from Veilby, dwelt a cattle-farmer, one Morten Burns, who, by means anything but honest and honorable, had acquired considerable property, and who was in ill repute as a reckless self-seeker, and oppressor of the poor. This man Morten thought fit to pay court to the pastor's daughter, but his suit was rejected by both parent and child; and either the refusal, or the manner of it, so irritated the suitor that he swore secretly to be revenged on both.

Some months later, when the short-lived suit had been forgotten, the pastor, being in want of a farm servant, engaged Niels Burns, a poor brother of the rich Morten, the discarded lover. Niels soon showed himself to be an utterly worthless fellow, lazy, impudent, and overbearing; and the result was a constant recurrence of quarrels and mutual recriminations between him and his master. Sören on more than one occasion gave the fellow a thrashing, which did not at all tend to improve the relations between them. These relations, however, were destined to come to a speedy close. The pastor had set Niels to dig a piece of ground in the garden, but on coming out he found him not digging, but leisurely resting on his spade and cracking nuts which he had plucked, his work being left undone. The pastor scolded him angrily; the man retorted that it was no business of his to dig in the garden; at which Sören struck him twice in the face, and the fellow, throwing down the spade, retaliated with a volley of abuse. Thereupon the old man lost all self-control, and seizing the spade, he dealt the fellow several blows with it. Niels fell to the earth like one dead; but when his master in great alarm raised him up he broke away, leaped through the hedge, and made off into the neighboring wood. From that time he was seen no more, and all inquiries after him proved vain. The above was the pastor's account of the facts.

Ere long strange rumors began to circulate in the neighborhood, and, as a matter of course, they reached the pastor's ears. Morten Burns was known to have said that "he would make the parson produce his brother even if he had to dig him out of the earth." Sören was intensely pained at the calumny implied, and instituted at his own expense a quiet search after the missing man—a search which failed altogether. Even before that failure was known, Morten Burns, in fulfillment of his threat, applied to the district magistrate, taking with him as witnesses one Larsen, a cottager, and a laborer's widow and daughter, on the strength of whose testimony he declared his suspicion that the pastor had slain his brother. The magistrate represented to him the risk he ran in making so serious a charge against the clergyman, and advised him to weigh the matter well before it was too late. But Morten persisted in his design, and the statements of the witnesses were taken down. The widow Karsten deposed, that on the very day when Niels Bruns was said to have fled from the parsonage, she and her daughter Else had passed by the pastor's garden about the hour of noon. When they were nearly in front of the hedge which encloses it on the eastern side, they heard some one calling Else. It was Niels, who was on the other side of the hazel bushes, and who now bent back the branches, and asked Else if she would have some nuts. She took a handful, and then asked him what he was doing there? He answered, that the pastor had ordered him to dig, but that the job did not suit him, and he preferred cracking nuts. Just then they heard a door in the house open, and Niels said, "Now, listen, and you shall hear a preachment." Directly after they heard (they could not see, because the hedge was too high and too thick) how the two quarreled, and how the one paid the other in kind. At last they heard the pastor cry, "I will beat thee, dog, until thou liest dead at my feet!" Whereupon there were sounds as of blows, and then they heard Niels calling the pastor a rogue and a hangman. To this the pastor made no reply; but they heard two blows, and they saw the iron blade of a spade and part of the handle swing twice above the hedgerow, but in whose hands they could not discern. After this all was quiet in the garden, and, somewhat alarmed and excited, the widow and her daughter hurried on their way.

Larsen disposed that on the evening of the day following that of the disappearance of Niels, as he was returning home very late from Tolstrup, and was passing along the footpath which flanks the southern side of the pastor's garden, he heard from within the garden the sound of some one digging the earth. At first he was rather startled; but seeing that it was clear moonlight, he determined to find out who it was that was working in the garden at that late hour; whereupon he slipped off his wooden shoes, climbed up the hedge, and parted the tops of the hazel bushes so as to enable himself to see. Then he saw the pastor in the green dressing-gown he usually wore, and with a white night-cap on his head, busied in leveling the earth with a spade; but more than this he did not see, for the pastor turned suddenly round as if some sound had struck his ear, and witness being afraid of detection, let himself down, and ran away.

When the witnesses had thus disposed, Morten demanded that the parson should be arrested. Wishing to avoid such a scandal if possible, the magistrate, who was a friend of Sören's, proposed that they should go together to the parsonage, where they would probably receive a satisfactory explanation of the facts deposed to. Morten consented to this, and the party set out. On approaching the house they saw Sören coming to meet them—when Morten ran forward, and bluntly accused him of murdering his brother, adding that he was come with the magistrate to make search for the body. The pastor made him no reply, but courteously greeting the magistrate, gave directions to the farm servants, who now gathered round, to aid by all the means in their power the search about to be made. Morten led the way into the garden, and after looking round for some time, pointed to a certain spot and called upon the men to dig there. The men fell to work, and Morten joined them, working with a show of frantic eagerness. When they had dug to a little depth the ground proved so hard that it was evident it had not been broken up for a long while. Sören had looked on quite at ease, and now he said to Morten, "Slanderer, what have you got for your pains?" Instead of replying, Morten turned to Larsen, and asked him where it was that he had seen the parson digging. Larsen pointed to a heap of cabbage stalks, dried haulms, and other refuse, and said he thought that was the place. The rubbish was soon removed, and the men began digging at the soil beneath. They had not dug long, when one of them cried out, "Heaven preserve us!" and as all present crowded to look, the crown of a hat was visible above the earth. "That is Niel's hat!" cried Morten, "I know it well—here is a security we shall find him! Dig away!" he shouted with fierce energy, and was almost as eagerly obeyed. Soon an arm appeared, and in a few minutes the entire corpse was disinterred. There could be no doubt that it was the missing man. The face could not be recognized, for decomposition had commenced, and the features had been injured by blows; but all his clothes, even unto his shirt with his name on it, were identified by his fellow servants; even a leaden ring in the left ear of the corpse was recognized as one which Niels had worn for years.

There was no alternative but to arrest the pastor on the spot—indeed, he willingly surrendered himself, merely protesting his innocence. "Appearances are against me," he said; "surely this must be the work of Satan and his ministry; but He still lives who will at his pleasure make my innocence manifest. Take me to prison; in solitude and in chains I will await what He in his wisdom shall decree."

The pastor was removed to the goal at Grenaee the same night, and on the following day came the judicial examination. The first three witnesses confirmed their former statements on oath. Moreover, there now appeared three additional witnesses, viz: the pastor's two farm servants and the dairymaid. The two former explained how on the day of the murder they had been sitting near the open window in the servant's room, and had heard distinctly how the pastor and the man Neils were quarreling, and how the former had cried out, "I will slay thee, dog! thou shalt lie dead at my feet!" They added that they had twice before heard the pastor threaten Niels with the like. The dairymaid deposed that on the night when Larsen saw the pastor in the garden, she was lying awake in bed, and heard the door leading from the passage into the garden creak; and that when she rose and peeped out, she saw the pastor, in his dressing-gown and night-cap, go out into the garden. What he did there she saw not; but about an hour afterwards she again heard the creaking of the door.

When asked what he had to say in his defense, the pastor replied solemnly, "So help me God, I will say nothing but the truth. I struck deceased with the spade, but not otherwise than that he was able to run away from me, and out of the garden; what became of him afterwards, or how he came to be buried in my garden, I know not. As for the evidence of Larsen and the dairymaid, who say that they saw me in the garden in the night, it is either a foul lie or it is a hellish delusion. Miserable man that I am! I have no one on earth to speak in my defense—that I see clearly; if He in heaven likewise remains silent, I have only to submit to His inscrutable will."

When, some weeks later, the trial came on, two more fresh witnesses were produced. They declared that on the oft-mentioned night they were proceeding along the road which runs from the pastor's garden to the wood, when they met a man carrying a sack on his back, who passed them and walked on in the direction of the garden. His face they could not see, inasmuch as it was concealed by the overhanging sack; but as the moon was shining on his back, they could plainly descry that he was clad in a pale green coat and a white night-cap. He disappeared near the pastor's garden hedge. No sooner did the pastor hear the evidence of the witness to this effect than his face turned an ashy hue, and he cried out in a faltering voice, "I am fainting!" and was so prostrated in body that he had to be taken back to prison. There, after a period of severe suffering, to the intense astonishment of every one, he made, to his friend, the district magistrate who had first arrested him, the following strange confession:—"From my childhood, as far back as I can remember, I have ever been passionate, quarrelsome, and proud—impatient of contradiction, and ever ready with a blow. Yet have I seldom let the sun go down on my wrath, nor have I borne ill-will to any one. When but a lad I slew in anger a dog which one day ate my dinner, which I had left in his way. When, as a student, I went on foreign travel, I entered, on slight provocation, into a broil with a German youth in Leipsic, challenged him, and gave him a wound that endangered his life. For that deed, I feel it, I merited that which has now come upon me after long years; but the punishment falls upon my sinful head with tenfold weight now that I am broken down with age, a clergyman, and a father. Oh, Father in heaven! it is here that the wound is sorest."

After a pause of anguish, he continued: "I will now confess the crime which no doubt I have committed, but of which I am, nevertheless, not fully conscious. That I struck the unhappy man with the spade I know full well, and have already confessed; whether it were with the flat side or with the sharp edge I could not in my passion discern; that he then fell down, and afterwards again rose up and ran away—that is all that I know to a surety. What follows—heaven help me!—four witnesses have seen; namely, that I fetched the corpse from the wood and buried it; and that this must be substantially true I am obliged to believe, and I will tell you wherefore. Three or four times in my life, that I know of, it has happened to me to walk in my sleep. The last time (about nine years ago), I was next day to preach a funeral sermon over the remains of a man who had unexpectedly met with a dreadful death. I was at a loss for a text, when the words of a wise man among the ancient Greeks suddenly occurred to me, 'Call no man happy until he be in his grave.' To use the words of a heathen for the text of a Christian discourse, was not, methought, seemly; but I then remembered that the same thought, expressed in well-nigh the same terms, was to be met with somewhere in the Apocrypha. I sought, and sought, but could not find the passage. It was late, I was wearied by much previous labor; I therefore went to bed, and soon fell asleep. Greatly did I marvel the next morning when, on arising and seating myself at my writing desk, I saw before me, written in large letters in a piece of paper, 'Let no man be deemed happy before his end cometh (Syrach xi. 34).' But not this alone; I found likewise a funeral discourse—short, but as well written as any I had ever composed—and all in my own handwriting. In the chamber none other than I could have been. I knew, therefore, who it was that had written the discourse; and that it was no other than myself. Not more than half a year previous, I had, in the same marvelous state, gone in the night time into the church, and fetched away a handkerchief which I had left in the chair behind the altar. Mark now—

when the two witnesses this morning delivered their evidence before the court, then my previous sleep-walkings suddenly flashed across me; and I likewise called to mind that in the morning after the night during which the corpse must have been buried, I had been surprised to see my dressing-gown lying on the floor just inside the door, whereas it was always my custom to hang it on a chair by my bedside. The unhappy victim of my unbridled passion must, in all likelihood, have fallen down dead in the wood; and I must in my sleep-walking have followed him thither. Yes—the Lord have mercy!—so it was, so it must have been."

On the following day sentence of death was passed upon the prisoner—a sentence which many felt to be too severe, and which led to a friendly conspiracy on his behalf; and had it not been for his own refusal to be a party to anything unlawful, he might have escaped. The jailer was gained over, and a fisherman had his boat in readiness for a flight to the Swedish coast, where he would have been beyond the reach of danger. But Sören Qvist refused to flee. He longed, he said, for death; and he would not add a new stain to his reputation by a furtive flight. He maintained his strength of mind to the last, and from the scaffold he addressed to the bystanders a discourse of much power, which he had composed in prison during his last days. It treated of anger and its direful consequences, with touching allusions to himself and the dreadful crime to which his anger misled him. Thereafter, he doffed his coat, bound with his own hands the napkin before his eyes, and submitted his neck to the executioner's sword.

One-and-twenty years after the pastor, Sören Qvist of Veilby, had been accused, tried, condemned, and executed for the murder of his serving-man, an old beggarman applied for alms to the people of Aalsöe, the parish adjoining to Veilby. Suspicions were aroused by the exact likeness the beggarman bore to Morten Bruns, of Ingvorstrup, who had lately died, and also by the curious and anxious inquiries the man made concerning events long past. The pastor of Aalsöe, who had buried Morten Bruns, took the vagabond to his parsonage, and there the fellow, all unconscious of the portentous nature of the admission, acknowledged that he was Niels Bruns, the very man for whose supposed murder the pastor had suffered the shameful death of a criminal. Had his brother Morten survived him, it is pretty certain the truth, concealed so long, had never been known, as Niels had only returned to the district in the hope of profiting by Morten's death, the news of which had accidentally reached him. He professed—and, indeed, plainly experienced—the utmost horror on hearing the dreadful history of the pastor's cruel fate. It was all Morten's doing, he said; but he was so overcome by the terrible narrative that he could scarcely gather strength to reply to the questions put to him. The result of his exam ination and confession may be summed up very briefly. Morten had conceived a mortal hatred of Sören Qvist from the time that he refused him his daughter, and had determined on revenge. It was he who compelled Niels to take service with the pastor; he had spurred him on to the repeated offenses, in the expectation that violence would result, owing to the pastor's hasty temper; and had carefully nursed the feud which soon arose between master and man. Niels told him daily all that took place. On leaving the garden on that fatal day, he had run over to Ingvorstrup to acquaint his brother with what had happened. Morten shut him up in a private room that no one might see him. Shortly after midnight, when the whole village was asleep, the two brothers went to a place where the roads cross each other, and where two days previously a suicide had been buried—a young man of about

Niels' age and stature. In spite of Niels' reluctance and remonstrance they dug up the corpse and took it into Morten's house. Niels was made to strip and don a suit of Morten's, and the corpse was clad, piece by piece, in Niels' cast-off clothes, even to the very ear-ring. Then Morten battered the dead face with a spade, and hid it in a sack until the next night, when they carried it into the wood by Veilby parsonage. Niels asked what all these preparations meant. Morten told him to mind his own business, and to go and fetch the parson's green dressing-gown and cap. This Niels refused to do, whereupon Morten went and fetched them himself.* "And now," he said to his brother, "you go your way. Here is a purse with a hundred dollars—make for the frontier, where no one knows thee; pass thyself under another name, and never set thy foot on Danish soil again as thou wouldst answer it with thy life!" Niels did as he was commanded, and parted from Morten forever. He had enlisted for a soldier, had suffered great hardships, had lost a limb, and had returned to his native place a mere wreck.

* It was not the custom in Jutland, in those days—it is hardly the custom now—to lock up the house at night.

V.

Thomas Geddely was a waiter in a public house kept by a Mrs. Williams at York, and much frequented. The landlady was a bustling woman, a favorite with her customers, and had the reputation of being well-to-do. One morning it was found that her scrutoire had been broken open and rifled of a considerable sum; and as on that same morning Thomas Geddely did not make his appearance, everybody concluded that he was the robber. A year afterwards, or thereabouts, a man came to York who, under the name of James Crow, plied for employment as a porter, and thus picked up a scanty living for a few days. Meanwhile, from his unlucky likeness to Geddely he began to be mistaken for the thief. Many people addressed him as Tom Geddely, and when he declared that he did not know them, that his name was James Crow, and that he had never lived in York before, they would not believe him, and attributed his denial to his natural desire to escape the consequences of the robbery he had committed at the public house.

When subsequently his mistress was sent for, she singled him out from a number of people, and calling him Geddely, upbraided him with his ingratitude, and charged him with robbing her. When dragged before the justice of the peace, and examined in his presence, the man affirmed, as stoutly as any man could, that his name was not Geddely, that he had never known any person of that name, that he had never in his life lived in York before, and that his name was James Crow. He could not, however, get any one else to substantiate his affirmations; he could give but a poor account of himself, but was forced to admit that he led a vagabond life—and as the landlady and others swore positively to his person, he was committed to jail at York Castle to await his trial at the next assizes. When, in due time, the trial came on, he pleaded "not guilty," and denied as before that he was the person he was taken for; but the landlady of the inn and several other witnesses swore positively that he was the identical Thomas Geddely who was waiter when she was robbed; while a servant girl deposed that she had seen him on the very morning of the robbery in the room where the scrutoire was broken open, with a poker in his hand. As the prisoner had nothing to urge against the evidence but a simple denial, and as he could not prove an *alibi*, he was found guilty of the robbery, was condemned to death, and executed. He persisted to his latest breath in affirming that he was not Thomas Geddely, and that his name was Crow.

The truth of the poor fellow's declaration was established all too late. Not long after Crow's unjust punishment, the real Thomas Geddely, who, after the robbery, had fled from York to Ireland, was taken up in Dublin for a crime of the same stamp, and there condemned and executed. Between his conviction and execution, and again at the fatal tree, he confessed himself to be the very Thomas Geddely who had committed the robbery at York for which the unfortunate James Crow had suffered. A gentleman, a native of York, who happened to be at Dublin at the time of Geddely's trial and execution, and who knew him when he lived with Mrs. Williams, declared that the resemblance between the two men was so remarkable that it was next to impossible to distinguish their persons assunder.

VI.

One of the most lamentable cases of mistaken identity was that of Lesurques, the history of which may be summed up as follows :

In the month of April, 1796, a young man named Joseph Lesurques arrived in Paris from Douai, his native town. He was thirty-three years of age, and possessed a fortune equal to six hundred pounds a year. He hired apartments, and made preparations for residing permanently in Paris. One of his first cares was to repay one Guesno, of Douai, two thousand francs he had borrowed of him. On the following day Guesno invited Lesurques to breakfast. They accordingly went to a refreshment room, in company with two other persons, one of whom, named Couriol, happened to call just as they were sitting down to table. After breakfast they proceeded to the Palais Royal, and having taken coffee, separated. Four days afterwards, four horsemen, mounted on hired horses, were seen to drive out of Paris. They all wore long cloaks and sabres hanging from the waist. One of the party was Couriol.

Between twelve and one o'clock the four horsemen arrived at the village of Mongeron, on the road to Melun. There they dined, and then proceeded at a foot pace towards Lieursaint. They reached Lieursaint about three in the afternoon, and made a long halt at the inn, amusing themselves with billiards, and one of them having his horse shod. At half-past seven they remounted and rode off towards Melun. About an hour later the mail courier from Paris to Lyons arrived to change horses. It was then half-past eight, and the night had been for some time dark. The courier, having changed horses, set out to pass the long forest of Leuart. The mail at this period was a sort of post-chaise, with a large trunk behind containing the dispatches. There was one place only open to the public, at the side of the courier; and the place was occupied on that day by a man about thirty years of age, who had that morning taken it in the name of Laborde.

The next morning the mail was found rifled, the courier dead in his seat, and the postilion lying dead in the road—both being evidently slain with sabres. One horse only was found near the carriage. The mail had been robbed of seventy-five thousand livres in silver and bank bills. The officers of justice soon discovered that five persons had passed through the barrier on their way to Paris between four and five in the morning after the murders. The horse of the postilion was found wandering about the Place Royale; and they ascertained that four horses, covered with foam and quite exhausted, had been brought, about five in the morning, to a man named Muiron, Rue des Fosses, Saint Germain l'Auxerrois, by two persons who had hired them the day before. These two persons were named Bernard and Couriol. Bernard was immediately arrested; Couriol escaped. A description was obtained of the four who had ridden from Paris and stopped at Mongeron and Lieursaint, and also of the man who had taken his place with the courier under the name of Laborde. Couriol was traced to Chateau Thierry, where he was arrested, together with Guesno, the Douai carrier, and one Bruer, who happened to be in the same house. Guesno and Bruer proved *alibis* so clearly that they were discharged on arriving at Paris.

The magistrate, after discharging Guesno, told him to apply at his office the next morning for the return of his papers, which had been seized at Chateau Thierry; at the same time he had sent a police officer to Mongeron and Lieursaint to fetch the witnesses, of whom he gave a list. Guesno, being desirous to obtain his papers as soon as possible, left home the next day earlier than usual. On his way to the office he met Lesurques, who consented to accompany him. They went to the office, and as Daubenton, the Juge-de-Paix, had not yet arrived, they sat down in the antechamber to await his arrival. About two o'clock the Juge-de-Paix, who had entered his room by a back door, was thunderstruck on being told by the police officer who had come back with the witnesses, that two of them declared that two of the actual murderers were in the house. "Impossible!" he exclaimed, "guilty men would not voluntarily venture here." Not believing the statement he ordered the two women to be introduced separately; and examined each of them, when they repeated their statement and declared they could not be mistaken. Warning them solemnly that life and death depended on their truth, he had the accused brought into the room one by one, and after conversing with them sent them again to the antechamber, where they waited as before. When they had left the room the magistrate again asked the women if they persisted in their previons declarations. They did persist; their evidence was taken down in writing; and the two friends were immediately arrested. No time was lost in pushing on the prosecution. Seven persons were put upon their trial, amongst whom were Couriol, Madeline Breban (his mistress), Lesurques, and Guesno. Lesurques was sworn to most positively by several, as being one of the party, at different places on the road, on the day of the robbery and murder. It should be born in mind that the case was quite conclusive against Couriol. "I attended them (said one witness) at dinner at Mongeron; this one (Lesurques) wanted to pay the bill in assignats, but the tall dark one (Couriol) paid it in silver." A stable boy at Mongeron also identified him. A woman named Alfroy, of Lieursaint, and the innkeeper and his wife of the same place, all recognized him as of the party there—Lesurques declaring that he had never been present at either place. But the witnesses were positive, were unimpeached, were believed, and—were all mistaken. Lesurques and Couriol were convicted, Guesno, though as positively sworn to, proved his perfect innocence, and was acquitted. Lesurques called fifteen persons of known probity to prove an *alibi*, which was disbelieved in consequence of the folly of one of them, who falsified an entry in his book with the design of adding weight to the evidence in Lesurques's favor, but did it so clumsily that the falsification was discovered. Eighty persons of all classes declared the character of Lesurques to be irreproachable; but all was of no avail—he was condemned.

When the sentence was pronounced, rising from his place, he calmly said—"I am innocent of the crime imputed to me. Ah, citizens! if murder on the highway be atrocious, it is not less a crime to execute an innocent man."

Madeline Breban, though compromising herself, wildly exclaimed—"Lesurques is innocent—he is the victim of his fatal likeness to Dubosq."

Couriol then, addressing the judges, said—"I am guilty; I acknowledge my crime; my accomplices were Vidal, Rossi, Durochat, and Dubosq; but Lesurques is innocent."

After the sentence had been pronounced, the horror-stricken Madeline again presented herself before the judges to reiterate her declaration, and two other witnesses attested to her having told them so before the trial. The judges applied to the Directory for a reprieve; and the Directory applied to the Council of Five Hundred, requesting instructions for their guidance, and concluding with the emphatic question—"Ought Lesurques to die on the scaffold because he resembles a criminal?" The answer was prompt: "The jury had legally sentenced the accused, and the right of pardon had been abolished."

Left to his fate, poor Lesurques on the morning of his execution thus wrote to his wife:—"My dear friend, we cannot avoid our fate. I shall, at any rate, endure mine with the courage which becomes a man. I send some locks of my hair. When my children are older, divide it with them. It is the only thing that I can leave them."

Couriol had disclosed to Lesurques the history of Dubosq, and the fatal mistake which had been made, and accordingly, on the eve of his death, he had the following mournful letter inserted in the journals: "Man, in whose place I am to die, be satisfied with the sacrifice of my life; if you be ever brought to justice, think of my three children covered with shame, and of their mother's despair, and do not prolong the misfortunes of so fatal a resemblance."

On the 10th of March, 1797, Lesurques went to the place of execution dressed completely in white, as a symbol of his innocence. On the way from the prison to the place of execution, Couriol, who was seated in the car beside him, cried in a loud voice, addressing the people, "I am guilty; but Lesurques is innocent." On reaching the scaffold, Lesurques gave himself up to the executioners, and died protesting his innocence.

In consequence of his own misgivings, and of murmurs on the part of the public, Daubenton, the Juge-de-Paix, who had arrested Lesurques, and conducted the first proceedings, resolved to investigate the truth, which could only be satisfactorily done through the arrest and trial of the four persons denounced by Couriol as his accomplices. Two years elapsed in vain inquiries. At the end of that time, he discovered that Durochat—the man who, under the name of Laborde, had taken the place by the side of the courier—had been arrested for a robbery, and lodged in St. Pelagie.

When the trial of the villain came on, he was, through the exertions of Daubenton, recognized by the inspector of the mails as the man who traveled with the courier on the day of the assassination. When charged with the fact, he made at first some faint denials, and subsequently he confessed, relating the particulars of the crime, all which tallied with the statements made by Couriol. He stated that Vidal had projected the affair, and had communicated it to him as a *restaurant* in the Champs Elysees. The criminals were Couriol, Rossi, (*alias* Beroldy), Vidal, himself, and Dubosq. Dubosq had forged for him the passport in the name of Laborde, by means of which he easily procured another for

Lyons, to enable him to take his place in the mail. Bernard had supplied the four horses. They had attacked the carriage as the postilion was slackening his pace to ascend the hill. It was he (Durochat) who had stabbed the courier, at the instant that Rossi cut down the postilion with a sabre; Rossi had then given up his horse to him (Durochat), and had returned to Paris on that of the postilion. As soon as they arrived there, they all met at Dubosq's lodgings, where they proceeded to divide the booty. Bernard, who had only procured the horses, was there, and claimed his share, and got it. "I have heard," he added, "that there was a fellow named Lesurques condemned for this business; but, to tell the truth, I never knew the fellow, either at the planning of the affair, or at its execution, or at the division of the spoil."

Such was Durochat's confession as taken down in writing; he added a description of Dubosq, stating that on the day of the murder he wore a blonde wig.

Shortly after the arrest of Durochat, Vidal was also arrested. He was recognized by the witnesses and positively sworn to, but he denied everything, and was sent to the prison of La Seine. Towards the end of the year 1799, Dubosq, having been arrested for a robbery in the department of Allier, was recognized in the prison and brought to Versailles to be tried at the same time as Vidal before the criminal tribunal. It was seen by the registers that Dubosq was a thorough desperado; he had been sentenced to the galleys for life, but had escaped, and on four several occasions had broken prison. Like Vidal, he denied everything. Confined in the same cell with his old companion in guilt, Dubosq planned an escape; but this time he broke his leg in the attempt—Vidal alone getting clear away—to be retaken, however, after a brief interval, to be brought back to trial—and to execution.

Strange as it may seem, Dubosq had no sooner recovered from his fracture, than he found another opportunity of attempting an escape, and for the sixth time succeeded in breaking his bonds. As he could not live without rapine, however, he fell again into the hands of the police before the expiration of a year, and was brought before the tribunal at Versailles. The president ordered a blonde wig to be put on his head, and thus attired, he was recognized by the same witnesses who had sworn away the life of Lesurques, who now recanted their former testimony, and declared too late that they had been mistaken.

After the execution of Dubosq, in Febuary, 1802, there still remained one of the accomplices to be brought to justice. This man, Rossi, whose real name was Beroldy, was at length discovered near Madrid, and was given up to the French government. Unlike Vidal and Dubosq, he confessed his crimes, testifying the utmost remorse. In the declaration, which he confided to his confessor, he affirmed the entire innocence of Lesurques; but, for a reason which does not appear, made it a condition that the declaration should not be published until six months after his death.

According to law, the property of Lesurques had been confiscated on his conviction, and his widow and children reduced to indigence. One would have thought that a government which had erred so egregiously as to execute a man for a crime of which he was not guilty, would have been eager to make what atonement was possible to the family of the victim. Nothing of the sort. The widow and her advisers, relying on the confessions of the real criminals, and the retractions of the witnesses, applied for a revision of the sentence, so far as concerned Lesurques, in order to obtain a judicial declaration of his innocence and the restoration of his property. All their endeavors were vain.

The right of revision no longer existed in the French code. Under the Directory, the Consulate, and the Restoration, the applications of the widow and family were equally unsuccessful. All that they could obtain was the restoration, in the last two years of the elder Bourbons, of a part of the property sequestrated at the condemnation of the unoffending husband and father.

VII.

On the 7th of February, 1851, in the dead of night, the house of David Williams, situated at Truasth, in the county of Brecknock, was broken open by forcing the shutters and window of an outhouse. Williams, an old man, who with his wife alone occupied the cottage, was alarmed by the noise, and going to the head of the stairs, saw by the light of a candle the person of a man whom he recognized as one Tom Williams, a blacksmith living in the neighborhood, and who had formerly done some work in the house. This was only for a moment, as the light was struck out, and the burglar attacked old Williams and his wife in the dark. However, they proved too strong for him, and compelled him to take to flight. Nothing was stolen, but the drawer of a dresser in the kitchen had been ransacked, and some papers of no value turned out of it. Tom Williams, the blacksmith, was tried at the following spring assizes at Brecon for the burglary, and as the old man, who had known him from his boyhood, swore to him positively, he was convicted, and sentenced to transportation. Happily for him, however, a person named Morris was present at the trial, who, on hearing the verdict, at once exculpated the convicted man, and directed the attention of the police to one Powell, as the real criminal. Strict inquiry was immediately instituted, the result of which was that Powell was committed. He was tried before the late Mr. Justice TALFOURD, and convicted on evidence perfectly conclusive. It seems old Williams had lent Powell six hundred pounds on mortgage, taking as security certain title deeds. Williams commenced proceedings to recover principal and interest, and Powell committed the burglary to possess himself of the documents; hence the ransacking of the dresser drawer in which he believed they had been deposited. The blacksmith was of course pardoned on the report of Mr. Justice TALFOURD, and was discharged in September. But the real criminal was also discharged, although his guilt was clear as the sun at noonday. The jury convicted him of breaking open the house "with intent to steal the title deeds;" the indictment charged his intent to be to "steal the goods and chattels." The Appeal Court held the conviction bad.

VIII.

A CURIOUS case of identification occurred about twenty years ago. This was an instance in which the guilt of a crime was brought home to the perpetrator through the identifying of a body after it had been separated limb from limb, submitted to chemical processes, and to the inordinate heat of a furnace, and mingled with the countless bones of anatomical subjects in their common burying-place. One Professor Webster was brought to trial for the murder of Dr. Parkman. It was shown that the professor had urgent pecuniary motives at the time when the crime was committed, to get Dr. Parkman out of the way. The prisoner had a residence at the Medical College, Boston. He made an appointment to meet the deceased at this place at two o'clock on Friday, the 23rd of November, 1849, in order to discuss certain money matters. Dr. Parkman was seen about a quarter before two o'clock apparently about to enter the Medical College, and after that was never again seen alive. The prisoner affirmed that Dr. Parkman did not keep his appointment, and did not enter the college at all on that day. For a whole week nothing was discovered, and when search was made the prisoner interfered with it, and threw hindrances in the way.

On the Friday week and the day following there were found in a furnace connected with the prisoner's laboratory in the college, fused together indiscriminately with the slag, the cinders, and the refuse of the fuel, a large number of bones and certain blocks of mineral teeth. A quantity of gold, which had been melted, was also found. Other bones were found in a vault under the college. There was also discovered in a tea-chest, and embedded in a quantity of tan, the entire trunk of a human body and other bones. The parts thus collected together from different places, made the entire body of a person of Dr. Parkman's age, about sixty years, and the form of the body when reconstructed had just the peculiarities shown to be possessed by Dr. Parkman. In no single particular were the parts dissimilar to these of the deceased, nor in the tea-chest or the furnace were any duplicate parts found over and above what was necessary to compose one body.

The remains were further shown to have been separated by a person possessed of anatomical skill, though not for anatomical purposes. Finally, three witnesses, dentists, testified to the mineral teeth found being those made for Dr. Parkman three years before. A mould of the doctor's jaw had been made at the time, and it was produced, and shown to be so peculiar that no accidental conformity of the teeth to the jaw could possibly account for the adaptation. This last piece of evidence was conclusive against the prisoner, and he was convicted. Without this closing proof the evidence would certainly have been unsatisfactory. The character of the prisoner, the possible confusion throughout the college of the remains of anatomical subjects, the undistinguished features, and the illusiveness of evidence derived from the likeness of a reconstructed body, were all facts of a nature to substantiate assumptions in favor of the prisoner's innocence. It is singular that the block of mineral teeth was only accidentally preserved, having been found so near the bottom of the furnace as to take the current of cold air, whose impact had prevented the thorough combustion that would otherwise have taken place.

IX.

On the 6th of August, 1660, William Harrison, who was steward to Lady Campden, a person of good estate in Gloucestershire, left his home in order to collect her rents. There happened to reside in the neighborhood a humble family of the name of Perry, a mother and two sons, Joan, John, and Richard, of whom Joan, the mother, bore but an indifferent character, and John, one of the sons, was known to be half-witted. It so happened that days and weeks elapsed, and yet Harrison did not return nor were any tidings heard of him. Of course, the population of the place became excited, and rumors soon became rife that he had been robbed and murdered. From the mission on which he was known to have left his home, and his prolonged absence, the suspicion was not unnatural. The alarm which ensued, and the numberless inventions which were circulated, are supposed to have bewildered what little intellect the poor idiot had, for he actually went before a justice of the peace, and solemnly deposed to the murder of Harrison by his brother Richard, while his mother and himself looked on, and afterwards joined in robbing the deceased of a hundred and forty pounds. On this the whole three were sent to prison, and at the following assizes were doubly indicted for the robbery and the murder. The presiding judge, Sir CHARLES TURNER, refused to try them on the murder indictment, as the body had not been found; they were, however, arraigned on the charge of robbery, and pleaded guilty on some vague superstition that their lives would be spared. While in confinement John persisted in the charge, adding that his mother and brother had attempted to poison him in the jail for peaching. When the next assizes came, Sir ROBERT HYDE, considering the length of time which had elapsed, and the non-appearance of Harrison, tried them for the murder. The depositions of John, and the plea on the indictment for robbery, were given in evidence, and the whole three were forthwith convicted. On the trial John retracted his accusation, declaring that he was mad when he made it, and knew not what he said. They all suffered death. The mother was executed first, it being alleged that she influenced her sons, and that they would never confess while she was living; they died, however, loudly protesting their innocence. But the disappearance of Harrison, the confession of John, and the plea of "guilty" to the indictment for robbery, seemed to invest the case with every human certainty.

After this poor, ignorant, and deluded family had lain in the grave for three years, the people of Gloucester were startled by the reappearance in their streets of the murdered Harrison! He accounted for his long absence thus, in a letter to Sir Thomas Overbury. On returning homewards after the receipt of Lady Campden's rents, he was set upon by a gang of crimps, who forced him to the seashore, where they hurried him on shipboard and carried him off to Turkey. They there sold him as a slave to a physician, with whom he lived for nearly two years, when, his master dying, he made his escape in a Hamburg vessel to Lisbon, and was thence conveyed to England.

X.

On the 6th of October, 1806, Thomas Wood, a young seaman, was tried at Plymouth by naval court-martial. The offense charged was an active participation in a mutiny and murder on board the "Hermione," in 1797. At the time of his trial, he was only twenty-five years old, and therefore somewhere about sixteen when the mutiny took place. There was but one witness against him; one, however, whose testimony had considerable weight—the master of the "Hermione." This person most positively identified him as one of those chiefly implicated, and as having gone, when on board his ship, by the name of James Hayes. The identification undoubtedly was strong; but still, considering the personal changes which generally take place between the age of sixteen and twenty-five, and after an interruption of nine years in the intercourse, scarcely strong enough to warrant a conviction. But all doubt of the prisoner's guilt vanished at once before the voluntary statement which he put in, in the form of a written document. "At the time," said the written statement, "when the mutiny took place, I was a boy in my fourteenth year. Compelled by the torrent of mutiny, I took the oath administered to me on the occasion. The examples of death which were before my eyes drove me for shelter among the mutineers, dreading a similar fate with those that fell if I sided with or showed the smallest inclination for mercy." To this frank and sweeping confession of his guilt he added a declaration of profound remorse for his crime, and wound up by throwing himself despairingly on the compassion of the court. The court found him guilty, passed upon him the sentence of death, and eleven days afterwards he was executed. In vain were all his supplications for compassion. In vain did his brother and sister interfere, proving, by a certificate from the Navy Office, that his written statement must have been a mere hallucination, seeing that the boy was at another place and in another ship when the crime was committed on board the "Hermione."

The subsequent establishment of this poor victim's innocence was most complete and satisfactory. The editor of a weekly journal, called the "Independent Whig," took up the matter very sternly, and denounced all the proceedings so indignantly from time to time that the members of the court-martial appealed to the Lords of the Admiralty for protection against the journalist. The Lords of the Admiralty responded to the appeal, and a prosecution was at once instituted. It was fortunate that the then law officers of the crown were Sir Arthur Pigott and Sir Samuel Romilly. These discreet men deemed it prudent to set on foot a strict inquiry into the facts before committing themselves to a public prosecution, "not, however," as Sir Samuel afterwards stated, "that either of us entertained any doubt as to the man's guilt." An inquiry was accordingly instituted by the solicitor of the Admiralty, the result of which was that Thomas Wood, who had been hanged for mutiny and murder, was proved to have been perfectly innocent, and was actually shown to have been doing his duty on board the "Marlborough" at Portsmouth at the very time that the crime was committed by the mutineers in the "Hermione." The reader naturally asks, How came Thomas Wood, if he was an innocent man, to confess himself guilty? The answer is not far to seek. Wood was a simple-minded Jack tar; he had no friends of any influence; he knew, or thought he knew, that no assertions of his would be of any avail against the positive evidence of the master of the "Hermione;" he therefore applied to another man to write a defense for him. Wood read the production of his comrade, and thinking it likely to excite the compassion of his judges, and that it would serve him better that a mere denial of the charges brought against him, adopted it. That the means chosen by his ignorant comrade for his defense proved his destruction, there can be no doubt. The confession acted as a bar to further inquiry, otherwise it is impossible to conceive that the certificate sent in by the brother and sister previous to the execution, and which showed the poor man's innocence, should not have been attended to. The truth was, that to all concerned in the condemnation of Thomas Wood, the facts were so clear, owing to the confession, that no regard whatever was paid to the exertions of his friends, and the official certificate was not merely slighted, it was probably never read.

XI.

On the first floor of a large hotel in the Rue Royale, at Paris, resided the Count and Countess de Montgomery. The Count was a personage of rank, and the possessor of considerable property, maintaining a numerous retinue of attendants, and an almoner, who formed part of the establishment. On the second and third floors of the same hotel the Sieur d'Anglade resided with his lady in a style of considerable respectability. The two families lived on the most amicable terms. It so happened that on one occasion the count and countess invited these neighbors to accompany them on a visit to one of their country seats. The invitation, at first accepted, was, for some unexplained reason, subsequently declined when the count and countess were just on the eve of their departure. Many of their numerous suite accompanied the family, and amongst these was the priest-almoner, Francis Gagnard. From some presentiment, it was said, pressing on the mind of the count, they returned to Paris the day before they were expected, and in the evening they received a visit from the d'Anglades. On the following day the unwelcome discovery was made that the count's strong box had been opened by a false key, and completely plundered. It' contents were thirteen small sacks with a thousand silver livres in each. In addition to these were near twelve thousand livres in gold, some double pistoles, a hundred louis d'or, of a new coinage called *au cordon*, and a pearl necklace worth four thousand livres. The whole had vanished.

The lieutenant of police having been consulted, at once pronounced the crime to have been perpetrated by some one within the house, and seems to have conceived and manifested a violent prejudice against the d'Anglade family. On observing this they immediately demanded that their apartments should be examined, and a strict search was made, their very beds having been ripped up, but nothing whatever was found to implicate any one in the floors which they inhabited. In an attic, however, which had been used as a kind of lumber-room, there were discovered, in an old trunk filled with parchments and rubbish, seventy louis d'or *au cordon*, wrapped up in a paper on which a genealogical table was printed, both of which Montgomery claimed, although the coin had no peculiar mark, and was in general circulation. From this moment the suspicions entertained by the lieutenant were adopted by the count. He loudly avouched the honesty of all his servants, and invidiously adverted to the theft of a piece of plate from the Sieur Grimandet, a former tenant, the d'Anglades at the same time living in the hotel. These suspicions were strengthened by the fact that it was known that d'Anglade had expensive habits, and that on their desiring him to count the coin he was observed to tremble. His trembling was the agitation of innocence under an accusation false but plausible. After this the small room in which the almoner, a page, and a *valet de chambre* slept, was subjected to a close search, and here, in a recess in the wall, were found five sacks containing a thousand livres each, and a sixth from which two hundred had been extracted. The d'Anglades were committed to prison, and it seems, by the law of France, the prejudiced police lieutenant who committed was the judge by whom they were to be tried. D'Anglade appealed to the parliament against this foul prejudgment, but he appealed in vain. It would appear that Count Montgomery had his misgivings, for he ordered his almoner, the priest Gagnard, to say a solemn mass at the church of Saint Esprit for the detection of the culprits; and accordingly the "holy man" so fervently implored the aid of the Divine Being that the prosecutor's conscience was at rest. The almoner was examined as a witness at the trial, though what was the nature of his evidence does not appear; whatever it may have been, satisfactory proofs were wanting to inculpate the accused. The public eye was upon the judge, and, without plausible proof, even a prejudiced judge shrank from pronouncing judgment. But he had an alternative, which at that time unhappily was legal. What the witnesses failed in proving, the torture might goad the accused to confess; they therefore put d'Anglade to the question, ordinary and extraordinary — they tormented him even to the verge of death, and then, covered over with wounds, his back dislocated, his whole frame shattered, all in ruins save a noble nature, they bore him back to prison beseeching God to manifest his innocence, and to pardon his inhuman persecutors and his inexorable judge. Although they failed to prove his guilt, they sentenced him to restore the amount which had been stolen, and to serve for nine years chained as a galley-slave. From this last degradation he was saved by death, for he sank in his dungeon at Marseilles, having received the sacraments. His poor widow and orphan, stripped of everything, even of the bed on which they lay, were banished from Paris and its precincts, and cast upon the world, forsaken and heartbroken.

After the death of d'Anglade and the utter desolation of his family, their innocence was clearly demonstrated. Inquiry was instituted in consequence of some letters which, at first anonymous, appear to have been written by an Abbé de Fontpierre, and the truth was brought to light. This son of the church and expounder of doctrine was a member of a thieves' society, and, as such, an associate of one Belestré, who was the principal in the crime. What motive impelled Fontpierre to write the letters—whether it was some quarrel with Belestré, or remorse at the fate of d'Anglade—does not appear. Belestre could not have accomplished the crime without assistance, and such was afforded him by Francis Gagnard, the inmate of Montgomery's house, and his trusted almoner, the reverend divine who actually celebrated the sacred ceremony at Saint Esprit for the discovery of the criminals. Gagnard and Belestré, both natives of the town of Mons, had been associated from infancy. The former was the son of a jailer; he had journeyed to Paris as an adventurer, and was eking out a mere subsistence by saying masses at Saint Esprit, when Montgomery admitted him on his establishment. The return he made was the furnishing his friend Belestré with wax impressions of all the keys he found there. It turned out that Belestré was a still greater villain than himself, having been in the army, from which he deserted after murdering his sergeant, and was afterwards prowling about the dens of Paris, alternately a gambler, a beggar, and a bully. Gagnard left the service of Montgomery after the conviction of d'Anglade, and following his criminal bent, soon found himself in prison, and, strangely enough, in the same cell with Belestré, arrested about the same time on a different charge. In the mean time the contents of the anonymous letters having much impressed the authorities, it occurred to them to interrogate the count's late almoner and his fellow prisoner as to the robbery in the Rue Royale. They were first examined apart, and an immediate prosecution was the result. The Abbé de Fontpierre gave most important evidence. Amongst other things he deposed, that being in a room adjoining one in which the accused was holding a revel, he heard Belestré say, "Come, my friend, let us drink and be merry, while d'Anglade is at the galleys." "Poor man," answered the almoner, "I can't help being sorry for him; he is a good sort of man, and was always obliging to me." "Sorry!" said the other, with a laugh, "sorry for the man who has saved us from suspicion and made our fortune!" A woman named De la Comble deposed that Belestré frequently showed her a beautiful pearl necklace, which he said he had won at play. Upon Belestré there was a gazette of Holland, in which, after reference to the d'Anglade case, there was a positive statement that the men who were really guilty of that robbery had been since executed at Orleans for another crime. Of this it was supposed he had himself procured the insertion in order to lull inquiry. Unfortunately, however, for him and his confederate, there was also found on him a document, in Gagnard's writing, alluding to the anonymous letters, and advising him by some means or other to quiet or to rid himself of the Abbé de Fontpierre. In addition to this it was shown that Gagnard, who on entering the count's service was almost destitute, and who could have saved but little from his salary, had on leaving it a profusion of money, which he lavished in feasting and debauchery. Belestré, also, was proved at the same period to have purchased an estate at Mons, where his father was a humble tanner. Madame d'Anglade completely cleared up the paltry suspicions by which her husband had been sacrificed; but it is needless to detail the particulars of the exculpation, as the criminals made a full confession of their guilt. Indeed, Gagnard went farther, and declared that, had he been closely interrogated during the first inquiry, such was his confusion, he must have admitted everything. But the mind of the judge was all intent on vindicating the prejudices in which he never should have indulged.

XII.

THERE lived in Paris a woman of fashion, known as Lady Mazel. Her house was roomy and lofty; on the ground floor was a large hall in which was a grand staircase; in a room opening into the hall slept the valet, whose name was Le Brun; the rest of this floor consisting of apartments in which the lady saw company. In the floor up one pair of stairs was the lady's own chamber, which was in front of the house, and was the innermost of three rooms from the grand staircase. The key of this chamber was usually taken out of the door and laid on a chair by the servant who was last with the lady, and who, pulling the door after her, shut it with a spring, so that it could not be opened from without. In this chamber, also were two doors — one communicating with a back staircase, the other with a wardrobe which also opened on the back stairs. On the second floor slept the Abbé Poulard; and on the third story were the chambers allotted to the servants; the fourth story consisted of lofts and granaries, whose doors were always open.

On the last Sunday in November, the two daughters of Le Brun, the valet, who were fashionable milliners, waited on the lady, and were kindly received; but, as she was going to church to the afternoon service, she pressed them to come again when she could have more of their company. Le Brun attended his lady to church, and then went to another himself, after which he went to several places, and having supped with a friend, he went home. Lady Mazel supped with the Abbé Poulard, as usual, and about eleven o'clock retired to her chamber, attended by her maids. Before they left her Le Brun came to the door to receive his orders for the next day; then one of the maids laid the key of the room door on the chair next it—they went out, and Le Brun following shut the door after him.

In the morning he went to market, made his purchases, and returning home transacted his business as usual. At eight o'clock he expressed surprise that his lady did not get up, as she generally rose early. He went to his wife's lodging, which was close by, told her he was uneasy that his lady's bell had not rung, and gave her some money which he desired her to lock up; he then went home again, and found the servants dismayed at hearing nothing of their lady. When one of them observed that he feared she had been seized with an illness, Le Brun said, "It must be something worse; my mind misgives me, for I found the street door open last night after all the family were in bed." They then sent for the lady's son, M. de Savoniere, who hinted to Le Brun his fear of an apoplexy. Le Brun replied that he feared something worse, and again mentioned his having found the street door open. A smith was sent for, the door was broken open, and Le Brun, running to the bed, after calling several times, threw back the curtains and cried out, "Oh, my lady is murdered!" He then ran to the wardrobe and took up the strong box, and finding it heavy, said, "She has not been robbed, how is this?" The body, on examination, showed no less than fifty wounds; they found in the bed a scrap of a cravat of coarse lace, and a napkin made into a nightcap, which was blood-stained, and had the family mark on it. From the wounds on the lady's hand, it appeared she had struggled bravely with the assassin; she could not ring for aid, the bell-strings being twisted round the tester, and thus out of her reach. A knife was found in the ashes almost consumed by the fire; the key of the chamber had been taken from the chair; but there were no marks of violence on any of the doors, nor were there any indications of a robbery, as a large sum of money and all the lady's jewels were found in the strong box and other places.

On being examined, Le Brun stated that after he left the maids on the stairs, he went down into the kitchen, and, sitting down by the fire, he fell asleep; that he slept, as he thought, about an hour, and going to lock the street door, he found it open; that he locked it, and took the key with him to his chamber. When searched, there was found in his pocket a key, the wards of which had been enlarged by filing, and which was found to open the street door, the antechamber, and both the doors in Lady Mazel's chamber. On trying the bloody nightcap on Le Brun's head, it was found to fit him exactly, whereupon he was committed to prison.

At the trial, it appeared that the lady had been murdered by some persons who had been admitted by Le Brun for the purpose. He could not himself have done it, because there was no blood upon his clothes, nor any scratch on his person, as there must have been on the murderer from the victim's struggling. But that Le Brun had let him in seemed clear. None of the locks were forced, and his story of finding the street door open, the circumstances of the key and the nightcap, also of a ladder of ropes being found in the house, which might be supposed to be laid there by Le Brun to take off the attention from himself, were all interpreted as proofs of his guilt. It was inferred that he had an accomplice, because part of the cravat found in the bed was discovered not to be his, *but the maids deposed that they had washed such a cravat for one Berry, who had been a footman to the lady, and who was turned away about four months before for robbing her.* There was also found in the loft at the top of the house, under some straw, a shirt very bloody, but which evidently had never belonged to Le Brun. The accused had nothing to oppose to these strong circumstances but his long and faithful service, and his uniformly good character. It was resolved to put him to the torture in order to discover his accomplices. This was done with such severity that he died in a few days of the injuries he received, declaring his innocence with his dying breath.

Poor Le Brun had scarcely been dead a month, when there came information from the provost of Sens, that a dealer in horses had lately set up there by the name of John Garlet, but whose real name was found to be Berry, and that he had been a footman in Paris. In consequence of this, he was taken up, and the suspicion of his guilt was increased by his attempting to bribe the officers. On searching him, a gold watch was found, which proved to be Lady Mazel's. A person in Paris swore to seeing him go out of Lady Mazel's, the night she was murdered; and a barber swore to shaving him next morning, when, on his remarking to his customer that his hands were very much scratched, Berry said he had been killing a cat. His guilt being evident, he was condemned to the torture, and afterwards to be broken alive on the wheel. Under the torture, he made, as many others have done, a false confession, declaring that at the instigation of Madame de Savoniere, Lady Mazel's daughter, he and Le Brun had undertaken to rob and murder the lady, and that Le Brun murdered her while he guarded the door to prevent surprise. But when brought to the place of execution, he recanted what he had said against Le Brun and Madame de Savoniere, and confessed "that he came to Paris on the Wednesday before the murder was committed. On the Friday evening he went into the house, and unperceived, got into one of the lofts, where he lay till Sunday morning, subsisting on apples and bread, which he had in his pockets; that about eleven o'clock on Sunday morning, when he knew the lady had gone to church, he stole down to her chamber, and the door being open, he tried to get under the bed; but it being too low, he returned to the loft, pulled off his coat and waistcoat, and returned to the chamber a second time, in his shirt. He then got under the bed, where he continued till the afternoon, when Lady Mazel went to church; that knowing she would not come back soon, he left his hiding-place, and being incommoded with his hat, he threw it under the bed, and made a cap of a napkin which lay on a chair, secured the bell-strings, and then sat down by the fire, where he continued till he heard her coach drive into the courtyard, when he again got under the bed and remained there; that Lady Mazel having been in bed about an hour, he got from under it, and demanded her money; she began to cry out, and attempted to ring, upon which he stabbed her, and she resisting with all her strength, he repeated the stabs till she was dead; that he then took the key of the wardrobe cupboard from the bed's head, opened the cupboard, found the key of the strong box, opened it and took out all the gold he could find, to the amount of about six hundred livres;

that he then locked the cupboard, and replaced the key at the bed's head, threw his knife into the fire, took his hat from under the bed, left the napkin in it, took the key of the chamber from the chair, and let himself out; went to the loft, where he pulled off his shirt and cravat, and leaving them there, put on his coat and waistcoat, and stole softly down stairs; and finding the street door only on the single lock, he opened it, went out, and left it open; that he had brought a rope ladder to let himself down from a widow if he had found the street door double locked, but finding it otherwise, he left the rope ladder at the bottom of the stairs, where it was found."

Thus was this foul mystery cleared up—and thus were all the circumstances which appeared against Le Brun accounted for, consistently with his innocence. Le Brun perished, as d'Anglade had perished, through the headlong precipitancy of the criminal court and the judge.

XIII.

A MOST melancholy case of circumstantial evidence happened in London, in the year 1815, the particulars of which must yet dwell in the memories of many still living. Eliza Fenning was a servant girl, very young, and said to be very beautiful, living in Chancery Lane. She was but twenty-one years of age, the dutiful and only child of respectable parents, then alive. She was tried at the Old Bailey, in the month of April, 1815, before the recorder of London, for the crime of administering poison to her master and mistress, and her master's father—a capital felony under Lord ELLENBOROUGH'S Act. The only evidence to affect the prisoner was entirely circumstantial. The poison was contained in dumplings made by her, but it was proved by the surgeon, who gave evidence at the trial, that she had eaten of them herself, and had been quite as ill as any of the persons whom she was supposed to have intended to poison. Further, her eating of them could not be ascribed to art, or to any attempt to conceal her crime, for she had made no effort whatever to remove the strongest evidence of guilt, if guilt there was. She had left the dish unwashed; and the proof that arsenic was mixed it it, was furnished by its being found in the kitchen on the following day, exactly in the state in which it had been brought from the table.

It is hardly conceivable that, such being the circumstances, a conviction could have been possible. "But," says Sir SAMUEL ROMILLY, from whose manuscript this account is condensed, "the recorder appeared to have conceived a strong prejudice against the prisoner; in summing up the evidence, he made some very unjust and unfounded observations to her disadvantage, and she was convicted." Petitions signed, not by hundreds, but by thousands, besought the throne for mercy. The master of the girl was requested to add his name to the petitioners on her behalf, but the recorder dissuaded him, and at his instance he refused. All intercession was fruitless, and Eliza Fenning was ordered for execution. She mildly, but earnestly, asserted her innocence to the last, and prayed to God some day to make it manifest. When the religious ceremonies were over, the sad procession moved towards the scaffold. As the last door was opening which still concealed her from the public gaze, Mr. Cotton, the ordinary, made a final effort: "Eliza, have you nothing more to say to me?" It was an awful moment, but her last words in this world were, "Before the just and Almighty God, and by the faith of the Holy Sacrament I have received, I am innocent of the offense of which I am charged." The door then opened, and she stood robed in white, before the people. Two old offenders were executed with her, "and," says a bystander, "as all three stood under the beam, beneath the sun, she looked serene as angel." The stormy multitude was hushed at once, and while all eyes wept, and every tongue prayed for her, she passed into eternity.

When the curtain had fallen upon this tragedy, the fury of the people knew no bounds, and the house of the prosecutor was protected only by the presence of a considerable force. The temper of the times was such that nothing could prevent a popular demonstration at the funeral, and a mournful and striking one it must have been. The broken-hearted parents led the way, followed by six young females clad in white, and then by eight chief mourners. At least ten thousand persons accompanied the hearse, and thus, every window filled, and every housetop crowded, they reached the cemetery of St. George the Martyr, where the remains of the innocent girl was interred.

Sir SAMUEL ROMILLY further states, that after Eliza Fenning's conviction, and while the error was reparable, "an offer was made to prove that there was in the house of Eliza's master, when the poisoning took place, a person who had labored, a short time before, under mental derangement, and who, in that state, had declared his fears that he should destroy himself and his family." This statement was made to the recorder himself, and evidence of its truth was offered, but that functionary affirmed that the production of any evidence of the kind would be wholly useless. That the crime was committed by a maniac, there can be but small doubt. The testimony of Mr. Gibson, who was then connected with the firm of Corbyn & Co., Holborn, is all but conclusive on the point. This gentleman stated that "about September or October, in the preceding year, a Mr. —— (the name, for obvious reasons, was not made public), called on me in Holborn. He seemed in such a wild and deranged state, that I took him into a back room, where he used the most violent and incoherent expressions—'My dear Gibson, do, for Heaven's sake, get me secured or confined, for if I am left at liberty I shall do some mischief; I shall destroy myself and my wife. I must and shall do it unless all means of destruction are removed out of my way; therefore do, my good friend, have me put under some restraint; *something from above* tells me I must do it, and, unless I am prevented, I shall certainly do it." Mr. Gibson felt it his duty to communicate this to the poor maniac's family, but they were heedless of the warning, and he was left at liberty.

XIV.

About the middle of the last century, Richard Coleman was indicted at the Kingston assizes, in Surrey, for the murder of Sarah Green. Coleman was a man of some education, was married and had several children, and was clerk to a brewer when the affair happened which cost him his life. One Sarah Green, a woman of a humble class, was attacked by three men, who maltreated her so cruelly that she afterwards died. These men had the appearance of brewers' servants,; and while she was under treatment in the hospital, she declared that a clerk in Berry's brewhouse was one of them, though it was not clear to whom she alluded. Two days after the transaction, Coleman went into an alehouse for refreshment, where he met with one Daniel Trotman, whom he knew. Having called for some spirits and water, Coleman was stirring it with a spoon, when a stranger who was present, asked him what he had done with the pig—alluding to a pig which had been lately stolen in the neighborhood. The retort led to a violent quarrel, in the course of which, the stranger insinuated that Coleman had been concerned in the murder of Sarah Green. Coleman answered the insinuation only by further aggravating his opponent. There was no breach of the peace, and the parties separated at length, with mutual ill-temper and personal abuse.

A day or two after this quarrel, Daniel Trotman and another man went before a magistrate in the Borough, and charged Coleman with the crime. The magistrate, not supposing that Coleman was guilty, sent a man with him to the hospital where the wounded woman lay, and a person pointing out Coleman, asked her if he was one of the persons who assailed her. She said she believed he was, but as she declined to swear positively to his having any concern in the affair, the magistrate, Justice Clarke, admitted him to bail. A short time afterwards Coleman was again taken before the magistrate, when nothing positive being sworn against him, the justice would have absolutely discharged him; but Mr. Wynne, the master of the injured girl, requesting that he might be once more taken to see her, a time was fixed for that purpose, and the justice took Coleman's word for his appearance. He came punctually to his time, bringing with him the landlord of an alehouse where Sarah Green had been drinking on the night of the crime with the three men who were really guilty; and this publican, and other people, declared on oath that Coleman was not one of the party. On the following day, Justice CLARKE went to the hospital to take the examination of the woman on oath. Having asked her if Coleman was one of the men who had attacked her, she said she could not tell, as it was dark at the time, but Coleman being called in, an oath was administered to her, when she swore that he was one of the three assailants. Spite of her oath, the justice, who thought the poor girl not in her right senses, and was convinced in his own mind of the innocence of Coleman, permitted him to depart, on his promise of bringing bail the following day, to answer the complaint at the next assizes for Surrey; and he brought his bail and gave security accordingly.

Sarah Green dying in the hospital, the coroner's jury sat to inquire the cause of her death; and having found a verdict of willful murder against Richard Coleman and two persons then unknown, a warrant was issued to take Coleman into custody. Though conscious of his innocence, yet such was the agitation of his mind at the idea of being sent to prison on such a charge, that Coleman absconded, and secreted himself at Pinner, near Harrow-on-the-Hill. The king being then at Hanover, a proclamation was issued by the lords of the regency, offering a reward of fifty pounds for the apprehension of the supposed offender; and to this the parish of Saint Saviour, Southwark, added a further sum of twenty pounds. Coleman read in the "Gazette" an advertisement for his apprehension, but was still so thoughtless as to conceal himself, though perhaps an immediate and voluntary surrender would have been his wisest course. However, to assert his innocence, he caused the following advertisement to be printed in the newspapers:

"I, Richard Coleman, seeing myself advertised in the 'Gazette' as absconding on account of the murder of Sarah Green, knowing myself not any way culpable, do assert that I have not absconded from justice, but will willingly and readily appear at the next assizes, knowing that my innocence will acquit me."

The authorities, not choosing to wait for his promised appearance, however, made strict search after him, and he was apprehended at Pinner on the 22nd of November, and lodged in Southwark jail till the time of the assizes at Kingston, Surrey.

At the trial several persons swore positively that Coleman was at another place at the time the crime was committed; but their evidence was not believed, and he was convicted principally upon the evidence of Daniel Trotman, and the declaration of the dying woman. After conviction, Coleman behaved like a man possessed of conscious innocence, and betrayed no fear in dying for a crime which he had not com mitted. At the place of execution, he delivered to the chaplain who had attended him a paper, in which he declared, in the most solemn and explicit manner, that he was altogether innocent of the crime alleged against him. He was executed at Kennington Common, on the 12th of April, 1749—and died with perfect resignation, lamenting only the distress in which he should leave a wife and two children.

About two years after Coleman's death, it was discovered that three working brewers named James Welch, Thomas Jones, and John Nichols, were the persons who had actually occasioned the death of Sarah Green. These wretches had been intimately acquainted from their childhood, and had kept the murder a secret, till it was discovered in the following manner. Welch, and a young fellow named James Bush, were walking together in the neighborhood of Newington, when their conversation happened to turn on the subject of persons who had been executed for offenses of which they had not been guilty—"Among whom," said Welch, as if by a sudden impulse, "was Richard Coleman. Nichols, Jones, and I, were the persons who committed the murder for which he was hanged." Welch then went on to relate the circumstances of the crime—his companion listening to the disclosure with feelings that may be imagined. Bush scarcely credited the story thus abruptly communicated, and for a time said nothing about it to any one; at length, however, he told his father what he had heard, and his father meeting shortly afterwards with Thomas Jones, and willing to test the truth of so strange a tale, abruptly charged him with being one of the murderers of Sarah Green. Jones trembled and turned pale at the charge, but soon assuming a degree of courage, said: "What does it signify? The man is hanged, and the woman is dead, and nobody can hurt us." In consequence of this acknowledgment, Nichols, Jones, and Welch were apprehended, when all of them steadily denied their guilt. Nichols, however, subsequently turned against his companions, and was admitted as evidence for the crown.

The prisoners being brought to trial at the next Surrey assizes, were both of them convicted on the testimony of Nichols, and sentence of death was passed upon them. After conviction, they behaved with the utmost contrition, and made a full confession of their crime. They likewise signed a declaration which they begged might be published, containing the fullest assertions of Coleman's *innocence.*

XV.

Another case, in which an innocent man was convicted on the evidence of a dying person, was that of William Shaw, of Leith. Shaw was an artisan, and lived in that town respectably for his station in life, his family consisting but of an only daughter, who resided with him; she had formed an unfortunate attachment to a young man whom the father knew to be of bad character, and therefore sternly discountenanced his addresses. This gave rise to continual dissension, until, at length, it one day rose to such a height, that James Morrison, the tenant of an adjoining room, could not avoid overhearing the conversation. The voices of father and daughter were recognized, and the words, "cruelty," "barbarity," and "death," were over and over again angrily enunciated. The father at last left the room abruptly, locking the door behind him, and leaving the daughter a prisoner. After some little time, deep noises were heard from within, which gradually becoming fainter, the alarmed neighbors procured the assistance of a bailiff, and burst open the door. Ghastly, indeed, was the spectacle which presented itself. There lay the young woman on the floor, weltering in her blood—a knife, the instrument of her death, beside her. To the question whether her father had been the cause of her sad condition, she was just able to make a faint affirmative gesture, and expired. At this moment the father reappeared. His horror may be imagined; every eye was fixed on him, and some specks of blood upon his shirt-sleeves seemed to confirm strongly the dreadful accusation which his daughter's dying gesture had too clearly intimated. Vainly attempting to account for the stained sleeve by the rupture of some swathe with which he had bound his wrist, he was hurried before a magistrate, and, upon the depositions of all the parties, committed to prison upon suspicion. He was shortly after brought to trial, when, in his defense, he acknowledged his having confined his daughter to prevent her intercourse with Lawson, the young man to whom he objected; and that he had quarreled with her on the subject the evening she was found murdered, as the witness Morrison had deposed; but he averred that he left his daughter unharmed and untouched, and that the blood found upon his shirt was there in consequence of his having bled himself some days before, and the bandage becoming untied. These assertions did not weigh a feather with the jury when opposed to the strong circumstantial evidence of the daughter's expressions of "barbarity, cruelty, death," together with that apparently affirmative motion of her head, and of the blood so, as it seemed, providentially discovered on the father's shirt. On these severally concurring circumstances was William Shaw found guilty and executed.

After this unfortunate man had swung for weeks upon his gibbet—for he was gibbeted in chains, exposed to the four winds of heaven and the gaze of every passer-by—it was shown, beyond the possibility of donbt, that he was not merely guiltless, but that he had fallen a sacrifice to his regard for her whom he was accused of having murdered. The incoming tenant who succeeded Shaw, while rummaging in the chamber where Catherine Shaw died, discovered in a cavity on one side of the chimney, where it appeared to have fallen, a paper written by the wayward girl, announcing her intention of committing suicide, and ending with the words, "My inhuman father is the cause of my death;" thus explaining her expiring gesture. This document being shown, the handwriting was recognized and avowed to be Catherine's by many of her relatives and friends. It became the public talk, and the magistracy of Edinburgh, on a scrutiny, being convinced of its authenticity, ordered the body of William Shaw to be given to his relatives for interment. Willing to make some reparation to his memory, and to show some sympathy with the feelings of his relatives, they caused a pair of colors to be waved over his grave. It was all the compensation they could award.

XVI.

Jaques du Moulin, a French refugee, having brought over his family and a small sum of money, employed it in purchasing lots of goods that had been condemned at the custom-house, which he again disposed of by retail. As these goods were such as, having a high duty, were frequently smuggled, those who dealt in this way were generally suspected of increasing their stock by illicit means, and smuggling, or purchasing smuggled goods, under color of dealing only in goods that had been legally seized by the king's officers, and taken from smugglers. This trade, however, did not, in the general estimation, impeach his honesty, though it gave no sanction to his character; but he was often detected in uttering false gold. He came frequently to persons of whom he had received money, with several of these pieces of counterfeit coin, and pretended that they were among the pieces which had been paid him; this was generally denied with great eagerness, but, if particular circumstances did not confirm the contrary, he was always peremptory and obstinate in his charge. This soon brought him into disrepute, and he gradually lost not only his business, but his credit. It happened that, having sold a parcel of goods, which amounted to seventy-eight pounds, to one Harris, a person with whom he had before had no dealings, he received the money in guineas and Portugal gold, several pieces of which he scrupled; but the man having assured him that he himself had carefully examined and weighed those very pieces, and found them good, Du Moulin took them, and gave his receipt.

In a few days he returned with six pieces, which he averred were of base metal, and part of the sum which he had a few days before received of him for the lot of goods. Harris examined the pieces, and told Du Moulin that he was sure there were none of them among those which he had paid him, and refused to exchange them for others. Du Moulin as peremptorily insisted on the contrary, alleging that he had put the money in a drawer by itself, and locked it up till he offered it in payment of a bill of exchange, and then the pieces were found to be bad, insisting that they were the same to which he had objected. The man now became angry, and charged Du Moulin with intending a fraud. Du Moulin appeared to be rather piqued than intimidated at this charge; and having sworn that these were the pieces he received of Harris, Harris was at length obliged to make them good; but as he was confident Du Moulin had injured him by a fraud, supported by perjury, he told his story wherever he went, exclaiming against him with great bitterness, and met with many persons who made nearly the same complaints, and told him that it had been a practice of Du Moulin's for a considerable time. Du Moulin now found himself universally shunned; and hearing what Harris had reported from all parts, he brought his action for defamatory words, and Harris, irritated to the highest degree, stood upon his defense; and, in the mean time, having procured a meeting of several persons who had suffered the same way in their dealings with Du Moulin, they procured a warrant against him, and he was apprehended upon suspicion of counterfeiting the coin. Upon searching his drawers, a great number of pieces of counterfeit gold were found in a drawer by themselves, and several others were picked from other money, that was found in different parcels in his scrutoire; upon further search, a flask, several files, a pair of moulds, some powdered chalk, a small quantity of aqua regia, and several other implements, were discovered. No doubt could now be made of his guilt, which was extremely aggravated by the methods he had taken to dispose of the money he made, the insolence with which he had insisted upon its being paid him by others, and the perjury by which he had supported his claim. His action against Harris for defamation was also considered as greatly increasing his guilt, and everybody was impatient to see him punished. In these circumstances he was brought to his trial, and his many attempts to put off bad money, the quantity found by itself in his scrutoire, and, above all, the instruments of coining, which, upon a comparison, exactly answered the money in his possession, being proved, he was upon this evidence convicted, and received sentence of death.

It happened that a few days before he was to have been executed, one Williams, who had been bred a seal engraver, but had left his business, was killed by a fall from his horse; his wife who was then big with child, and near her time, immediately fell into fits, and miscarried. She was soon sensible that she could not live, and therefore sending for the wife of Du Moulin, she desired to be left alone, and gave her the following account:

That her husband was one of four, whom she named, that had for many years subsisted by counterfeiting gold coin, which she had been frequently employed to put off, and was therefore intrusted with the whole secret; that another of these persons had hired himself to Du Moulin as a kind of footman and porter, and being provided by the gang with false keys, had disposed of a very considerable sum of bad money, by opening his master's scrutoire, and leaving it there in the stead of an equal number of good pieces, which he took out; that by this iniquitous practice, Du Moulin had been defrauded of his business, his credit, and his liberty, to which in a short time his life would be added, if application was not immediately made to save him. By this account, which she gave in great agonies of mind, she was much exhausted, and having given directions where to find the persons whom she impeached, she fell into convulsions, and soon after expired. The woman immediately applied to a magistrate, and having related the story she had heard, procured a warrant against the three men, who were taken the same day, and separately examined. Du Moulin's servant steadily denied the whole charge, and so did one of the other two; but while the last was examining, a messenger who had been sent to search their lodgings, arrived with a great quantity of bad money, and many instruments for coining. This threw him into confusion, and the magistrate, improving the opportunity by offering him his life if he would become an evidence for the king, he confessed that he had been long associated with the other prisoners and the man that was dead, and he directed where other tools and money might be found, but he could say nothing as to the manner in which Du Moulin's servant was employed to put it off. Upon this discovery, Du Moulin's execution was suspended; and the king's witness swearing positively that his servant and the other prisoner had frequently coined in his presence, and giving a particular account of the process, and the part which each of them usually performed, they were convicted, and condemned to die. Both of them, however, still denied the fact, and the public were still in doubt about Du Moulin. In his defense, he had declared that the bad money which was found together was such as he could not trace to the persons of whom he had received it; that the parcels with which bad money was found mixed, he kept separate, that he might know to whom to apply if it should appear to be bad; but the finding of the moulds and other instruments in his custody was a particular not yet accounted for, as he only alleged in general terms that he knew not how they came there, and it was doubted whether the impeachment of others had not been managed with a view to save him who was equally guilty, there being no evidence of his servant's treachery but that of a woman who was dead, reported at second hand by the wife of Du Moulin, who was manifestly an interested party. He was not, however, charged by either of the convicts as an accomplice, a particular which was strongly urged by his friends in his behalf; but it happened that while the public opinion was thus held in suspense, a private drawer was discovered in a chest that belonged to his servant, and in it a bunch of keys, and the impression of one in wax; the impression was compared with the keys, and that which it corresponded with was found to open Du Moulin's scrutoire, in which the bad money and implements had been found. When this particular, so strong and unexpected, was urged, and the key produced, he burst into tears, and confessed all that had been alleged against him. He was then asked how the tools came into his master's scrutoire; and he answered, that when the officers of justice came to seize his master, he was terrified for himself, knowing that he had in his chest these instruments, which the private drawer would not contain, and fearing that he might be included in the warrant, his consciousness of guilt kept him in continual dread and suspicion; that for this reason, before the officers went up stairs, he opened the scrutoire with his false key, and having fetched his tools from his box in the garret, he deposited them there, and had just locked it when he heard them at the door.

In this case, even the positive evidence of Du Moulin, that the money he brought back to Harris was the same he had received of him, was not true, though Du Moulin was not guilty of perjury, either willfully or by neglect, inattention or forgetfulness. And the circumstantial evidence against him, however strong, would only have heaped one injury upon another, and have taken away the life of an unhappy wretch, from whom a perfidious servant had taken everything else.

XVII.

In the town of M——, in Germany, resided a goldsmith, named Christopher Ruprecht, aged upwards of sixty; rich, illiterate, quarrelsome, covetous; rude in speech, vulgar in his habits; whose chief indulgence consisted in frequenting low alehouses, and mingling in such haunts with the most disreputable among the lower classes of his fellow citizens. His selfishness and repulsive manners had alienated from him all his relations, with the exception of a sister, who resided with him, and a married daughter, who still continued, notwithstanding his peculiarities of temper, to visit him regularly, though as much from interest perhaps as affection.

The favorite resort of Ruprecht was a small alehouse of the meanest order, situated at the end of a dark winding lane, and receiving as a title, from its gloomy situation, and the orgies of which it was the scene, the emphatic monosyllable usually applied to the place of darkness. About half-past eight o'clock, on the evening of the 7th of February, 1817, the goldsmith repaired to this place according to his custom, took his seat among the circle which generally assembled round the inn fire on the first floor, and in his usual overbearing style, joined in the current conversation. In this manner the time was spent till past ten o'clock, when Ruprecht despatched the landlord to the ground floor for a further supply of beer. As the master of the house was reascending the stairs to the company with the liquor wanted, a voice from the passage or outer door below, was heard inquiring if Ruprecht was above; and on the landlord replying—without turning his head—in the affirmative, he was desired by the person below to tell the goldsmith to come down. On receiving the message, Ruprecht rose immediately, and left the room. A minute had scarcely elapsed afterwards, when the company heard distinctly a loud groaning from below stairs, followed by a sound as of a heavy body falling in the passage. All present, to the number of eleven, hurried down stairs, where they found the goldsmith lying near the house door, still alive, but covered with blood flowing from a large wound on his head. At a little distance lay his leather cap, which had been cut through by the blow. The only words which the wounded man uttered, when lifted up, were: "The villain—the villain with the axe!" and once afterwards, "My daughter, my daughter!" She was immediately sent for, but his mind apparently wandered, and he did not recognize her.

No trace of the author of the deed, or of any weapon, was visible in the neighborhood. On examination, the wound was found to be about four inches long, extending along the left side of the head from front to back, and deeper in the center than at the ends. From the force required to inflict such a blow, it was obvious that it must have been done outside the door, as the passage within was so low, that no weapon could have been raised sufficiently high to produce such an injury. After receiving it, the goldsmith must have been able to stagger into the passage before falling. On the left side of the door without, was a stone seat, two feet high, on which, it was supposed, the murderer must have taken his stand, awaiting his victim, and directed, from this position, the deadly stroke. Though Ruprecht's words implied that the weapon had been an axe, the medical inspector was of opinion that a saber, wielded by an experienced hand, was more likely to have been the instrument. The main hope of explaining this point, and of discovering the author of the deed, rested on the revelations which the goldsmith himself might be able to make. It was not, however, till the evening of the following day, that he appeared sufficiently in his senses to warrant the judge in commencing his examination. The wounded man's answers were given in monosyllables. He was asked:

"Who struck you?"

"Schmidt."

"What is this Schmidt—where does he reside?"

"In the Most." (The Most is a street of the town.)

"With what did he strike you?"

"A hatchet."

"How did you know him?"

"By his voice."

"Was he indebted to you?" Ruprecht shook his head.

"What was his motive?"

"A quarrel."

The wounded man was so much exhausted by these responses, that scarcely any other questions could be put to him, excepting the request, that he would again name the individual who had struck him. His repeated answer was, "Schmidt—woodcutter."

Who, then, was this Schmidt?—a name, it is to be observed, not less common in Germany than Smith is in England. It turned out that there were three Schmidts, woodcutters, in the town, two of whom were brothers, and lived in the Most, the street indicated by the goldsmith; while the third, Christopher Schmidt, lived in the street called the Hohen Pflaster. The brothers were usually named from their different heights, the Great Schmidt and the Little Schmidt, and they proved to be old acquaintances of Ruprecht, but to have recently ceased to be on familiar terms with him, chiefly because the Great Schmidt had given evidence against him in an action of damages. Regarding Christopher Schmidt, it was ascertained that, at a former period of his life, he had been imprisoned under a charge of accession to a robbery. Before proceeding to the arrest of any of these individuals, Ruprecht, whose skull had in the interval been trepanned, in order to raise the depressed bone, was again asked, at a favorable moment, a string of questions similar to the former, and gave the same responses, excepting in one important point. On being asked whether the Great or the Little Schmidt was the guilty person, he tried to speak, but failed. He was then asked if the Most was the street, but was silent. To the next question, "If the Hohen Pflaster was the man's residence?" he answered with difficulty, but distinctly, "Yes," and then relapsed into the state of insensibility which was common to him.

All three Schmidts being thus implicated in suspicion, they were taken into custody, for the purpose, in the first place, of being confronted with the wounded man, and to have the guilty individual, if possible, identified by him. But Ruprecht, though sensible, was unable to open his eyes, and the main object of the interview was thus defeated. The behavior of the suspected persons was, however, so very different, as to excite the strongest hopes that the matter would be cleared up. The brothers Schmidt were calm and composed on being brought into the goldsmith's presence; they spoke to him, called him by name, and expressed the greatest sympathy for his situation. Christopher Schmidt, on the contrary, was agitated and restless; when asked if he knew the person in bed, he first said he did not know him, and then that he did know him; first, that he remained in his mother-in-law's house on the night of the murder till eleven, and afterwards, that he was in his own house in bed at nine. He at the same time protested his entire innocence, and appealed to the testimony of his wife, his mother-in-law, and his neighbors. His agitation and contradictions drew the suspicion of all from the other Schmidts upon him, and he was committed by the judge to prison. All hope of further information from the victim himself, was put an end to by his death on the following day, the second from the accident.

Subsequent investigations tended to increase the suspicions against Christopher Schmidt, which his behavior on the first occasion had awakened. On inspecting his house, the handle of his axe, near the blade, was found to be streaked with blood! The truth of the report as to his former imprisonment he did not attempt to deny, but alleged that he had been merely made the innocent instrument of conveying stolen property from one place to another. On undergoing another examination, his contradictions were even more glaring than before. To the question, "How he came to know Ruprecht in bed, when he stated that he had never seen him before," he said that he knew him from having heard of his accident, and from being aware of the object of his own visit to the goldsmith's house. He stated that he had been with his wife and child to his mother-in-law's house, where they wrought at some in-door work, to save candles at home. It was impossible to ascertain from his answers the time at which he had come from his mother-in-law's house to his own. He first averred that he had come home with his child at nine, and that his wife had come an hour after him; then, that his wife had returned with him at ten o'clock; then that he was asleep, and did not know when she came; and made fresh contradictions, in short, with regard to time, at every query put to him. All these things—his variations, his agitation, his downcast and suspicious look, his previous imprisonment, the spots upon his axe, the expression of the dying man, which pointed most strongly to him—when taken together, formed a strong combination of circumstances against Christopher Schmidt. Indeed, his guilt was scarcely doubted of by any one.

On the other hand, after men's minds became capable of calmer reflection on the subject, the very grossness of these contradictions seemed to lead to the inference, that they arose from a deficiency of intellect, or from a mind disordered by temporary anxiety and fear, or from both causes, rather than from a desire to conceal the truth. The report of the neighbors, when their evidence was collected, corroborated this conjecture; his stolidity and dullness of intellect was such as to have acquired for him the common nickname of "The Sheep." He never was capable, it was found, of expressing himself clearly, and it followed that, under such circumstances as a charge of murder, this deficiency must evidently have been greatly aggravated. From such a character as this, the statement, illogical as it was, that he knew Ruprecht in bed from having heard of his accident, was natural enough. With regard to the contradictory representations regarding the hour of his return, the inconsistency might be in part explained away by supposing his wife to have first gone home with him, seen him to bed with the child, and afterwards to have returned to her mother's for a short period before she finally came to sleep in her own house. This was, in fact, substantially proved by subsequent investigations of Schmidt's mother-in-law and wife. They, with other witnesses, proved that the wife, having seen her husband home, went back to her mother's to finish some work, and after an hour or an hour and a half's stay, returned to her own domicile. It was remarkable, however, that these two witnesses differed considerably with respect to the hours at which these events took place. These discrepancies were held to arise from the fact, that the night in question was a long and dark one in February, and that no clocks were within reach of the parties. This gave a favorable color also to Schmidt's own inconsistencies as to time, particularly when taken in connection with the man's unquestionable stupidity.

But—admitting the wife's statement to be correct—Christopher Schmidt was left alone for an hour and a half at the very time the deed was comcommitted. The ale-house where it took place, however, was a mile and a quarter from Schmidt's dwelling; and to have been the actor in the deed, he must have sprung from bed at the moment of his wife's departure, hurried to the spot, committed the murder, and then been in bed a quarter of an hour afterwards. Was this energetic villainy likely to have been exhibited by one so slow and sluggish in intellect and behavior as Schmidt was proved to be? The thing was felt by all, on reflection, to be barely possible.

But, again, the blood on the handle of the axe? The accused, on being questioned respecting this, said, that if such stains existed, of which he knew nothing, they must have proceeded from a swelling in the hand—which he showed—that had burst some days before. The swelling, it was replied, is in the *right* hand, while the stains are upon the upper of the handle, which is always held in the *left* hand. "I am *left-handed*," said the accused; and on inquiry among his associates, it was found to be the case. Further examination, also, showed that the axe of Schmidt could not have been the instrument of death, the wound in the head being four inches long, while the axe's blade was barely three inches. A strong additional testimony in Schmidt's favor, was the discovery that he had actually been free of all guilt, as he had represented, on the occasion of his former imprisonment, and that his general character everywhere was that of a sober, industrious, peaceable man.

Thus, one by one, the grounds of suspicion which had at first appeared to be assuming so firm and compact a form, crumbled away, and, though not yet finally liberated, it was apparent to all that Christopher Schmidt would be acquitted. But, as the clouds of suspicion passed from Christopher, they gathered for a time round the heads of his namesakes, the Great and Little Schmidts of the Most. These men, it was recollected, knew

Ruprecht, which Christopher did not; they had, moreover, been actually placed in an inimical position with respect to the deceased. They had borne evidence against him, in an action instituted by two respectable surveyors, whose names the goldsmith had publicly vilified. Ruprecht had lost the cause, and had been sentenced to a short confinement on bread and water. At his liberation, he had set on foot an action of retaliation against the surveyors, which was still undecided at the time of the murder. Could the surveyors have made use of their former witnesses, the Schmidts, to rid themselves of their pertinacious opponent? The high character of the men rendered this supposition improbable; and after it had lived for but a short time on the public breath, it was completely extinguished by the coming forward of several witnesses, who spoke to the fact of the brothers Schmidt having come home early on the night of the goldsmith's death, and not having left the house till next morning.

While all grounds for suspicion to rest upon were thus disappearing as far as the parties first implicated were concerned, some new discoveries, or rather conjectures, were made, which drew the eyes of justice to an entirely different quarter.

Two other Schmidts, woodcutters also, were found out, not living in the town indeed, but in the suburbs. One of these men was woodman to Berenger, Ruprecht's son-in-law, and this circumstance seems to have originated a new train of thinking in the minds of the official persons of the town, though no ground of suspicion could be found against the newly discovered Schmidts. One of Ruprecht's first expressions, it will be remembered, after receiving the blow, was, "My daughter! my daughter!" These words had been naturally interpreted at the time into an expression of anxiety to see her, but circumstances subsequently emerging, seemed to render it doubtful whether his exclamation did not bear a less favorable meaning. The matrimonial life of Berenger and his wife had long been, it appeared, an unhappy one; Berenger had often made complaints against his wife to her father. Recently, some steps taken by the husband had ended in making the wedded pair's life a little more harmonious, but they had, at the same time, exasperated Ruprecht's mind in the highest degree against Berenger. A short time before his death, the goldsmith had been heard to call his son-in law a villain; and he had also for some time past entertained the resolution of making a will, leaving all to his daughter, and beyond her husband's control. This resolve he had announced to his daughter, about two months before his death, and also to his apprentice, Hogner. Nay, within a few hours of his accident, he had sent for Hogner to assist in arranging his papers, preparatory to the execution of the will on the following Sunday. This intention he had expressed in the hearing of of the maid servant. These remarkable circumstances directed the attention of justice to Berenger, who might have heard of the old man's determination; and a sufficient motive for a desire on his part to get rid quickly of the goldsmith would thus have been established.

Berenger, according to account, showed no emotion or sympathy on hearing of the accident, and his wife, it was said, showed also a want of feeling. One of her first concerns was to see whether her father had his keys about him; and having ascertained that he had, she took possession of and walked away with them. She had, besides, shown a strong anxiety to criminate one of the Schmidts, reporting several speeches against him, from her father's lips, which no one else had heard. Several other minor incidents seemed to bear against the Berengers. In interpreting her father's dying words with this view, it was thought that the old man, feeling himself struck with what he conceived to be an axe, would immediately revert in his mind to the woodcutters, the Schmidts, who had borne a part against him in the suit then pending, and which occupied at the time much of his attention. This was the sense now put upon the goldsmith's mention of the name of Schmidt.

Here also, however, as in the former cases, the grounds of suspicion vanished, one by one, into thin air. That the words "my daughter" bore no meaning unfavorable to the Berengers, was proved by the statement of Ruprecht's sister, that such was her brother's common expression when anything troubled him; it was also proved, on better inquiry, that Berenger's wife had shown deep feeling for her father, and had only taken away his keys on the surgeon suggesting that the murder might be a prelimary to robbery; it was, however, sworn by the wife, the apprentice, and the maid servant, that they had never spoken of the will—a thing, indeed, most unlikely for the wife to do, when she alone was to to be benefited by it; and, finally, there was distinct evidence that Berenger himself, at least, had not been the murderer, as, at the time of it, he was quietly seated in the parlor of the Golden Fish. By this and other evidence, the suspicion against the Berengers fell to peices.

Even after all these failures, the investigation was not abandoned. A soldier, who was indebted to Ruprecht, and who had been threatened by him, on the day of the accident, with hard measures, was the person next brought under examination. After the fabric of evidence in this case also had gathered strength, it was at once overturned by a clear proof of an alibi.

Here, at last, justice was obliged to give up the pursuit; nor has any light since been thrown on this strange story.

XVIII.

The following narrative, while it strikingly exhibits the fallible and uncertain nature of circumstantial evidence, affords also a convincing proof of the indispensable necessity of procuring medical testimony of the highest order, in all criminal cases relating to injuries of the person. The narrator, Mr. Perfect, a surgeon at Hammersmith, sent the statement to the editor of the *Lancet* (Mr. Wakley) in January, 1839:—

"It is now thirty years ago, that accidentally passing the Packhorse, Turnham Green, my attention was attracted by a mob of persons of the lowest order assembled around the door of that inn, who were very loud in their execrations against some person who was suspected of having murdered his brother; in corroboration of which, I was told that his bones were found near the premises where he formerly resided, upon view of which a jury was then sitting, after an adjournment from the day preceding. I found that two surgeons had been supœnaed to inspect the remains, and I had no doubt but that every information as to their character had been obtained; curiosity alone, therefore, induced me to make way into the room, where I found that the coroner, and, I believe, a *double jury*, were sitting for the second day, and were engaged in an investigation which tended to show that a farmer and market gardner at Suttoncourt Farm, had, a few years before, a brother living with him, who was engaged in the farm, but whose conduct was dissolute and irregular to a degree that often provoked the anger of his elder brother, and sometimes begat strife and violence between them; that the temper of the elder brother was as little under control as the conduct of the younger; and, in fine, that they lived very uncomfortably together.

"One winter night, when the ground was covered with snow, the younger brother absconded from the house (for they both lived together), by letting himself down from his chamber window; and when he was missed the ensuing morning, his footsteps were clearly tracked in the snow to a considerable distance, nor were there any other footsteps *but his own*. Time passed on, and after a lapse of some few years no tidings were heard of his retreat, nor perhaps have there ever been since. Some alterations in the grounds surrounding the house having been undertaken by a subsequent tenant (for the elder brother had then left the farm), a skeleton was dug up, and the circumstance appeared so conclusive that one brother had murdered the other, that the popular clamor was raised to the utmost, and a jury impanneled to investigate the case.

"After listening attentively to these details, I ventured to request of the coroner to be allowed to examine the bones, which I found were contained in a hamper basket at the further end of the room, and I felt much flattered by his immediate compliance, for he desired the parish beadle, who was in attendance, to place them upon the table; and having himself disposed them in their natural order, I found that they represented a person of short statute, and from the obliteration of the sutures of the skull, and the worn-down state of the teeth, must have belonged to an aged person. But what was my surprise when I reconstructed the bones of the skeleton, and found the lower bones of the trunk to be those of a female. I immediately communicated the fact to the jury, and requested that the two medical men who had before given their opinions might be sent for, one of whom attended, and without a moment's hesitation corroborated my report.

"I need not add that the proceedings were instantly at an end, and an innocent man received the *amende honorable*, in the shape of an apology, from all present, in which the coroner heartily joined. It has since been proved beyond all doubt that the spot where the bones were found was formerly the site of a large gravel pit, in which hordes of gipsies not only assembled, but occasionally buried their dead, and perhaps more skeletons are yet to be found in that vicinity."

XIX.

In the year 1841, at Gibraltar, there occurred one of those extraordinary cases, which show us how ineffectively the romancist, even when his imagination is strained to the uttermost, can portray the extremes of passion of which human nature is susceptible. A communication, bearing date Feberuary 20th, from the rock-built fortress which England keeps as a key to the Mediterranean, relates the following particulars:

A respectable merchant, named James Baxwell, born at London, had removed in early life to Gibraltar, induced partly by the circumstance of his being of the same religious persuasion to which the people of his adopted country belonged. For many years he occupied a small dwelling near the base of Mount St. Michael, so renowned for its caves and crystallizations. He carried on a successful traffic in all the articles of British manufacture introduced into Spain. He acquired, in truth, a very considereble fortune in this way. All the country knew that he had a large amount of treasure lying by him, not to speak of the capital belonging to him, which was embarked in commerce. His name was one of credit in all the principal houses of exchange in Europe.

James Baxwell had a daughter, an only daughter, aged seventeen, and of remarkable beauty. Her countenance and figure combined in a most agreeable manner the peculiar charms of the Englishman with the soft and languishing characteristics of the Spaniard. Young as she was, she had been for some two or three years an object of devoted admiration to all the youths around Gibraltar. At church they devoured her with their eyes; and many, many a one thought to himself that happy above all men would be he who could win the smiles of Elezia Baxwell. But Elezia bestowed her smiles upon no one. She seemed, to those whose involuntary sighs she excited, to carry maidenly modesty to freezing coldness. At mass, *her* eyes were ever bent upon her book, regardless of all the glances cast upon her by others.

Such was, at least, the case, till shortly before the events to be narrated. At length, however, Elezia did see one who awakened in herself some of the emotions which she had caused in others. At mass, one day, she observed the eyes of a young stranger fixed upon her with an expression of admiration and respect. To her he seemed a being superior to all the young men she had ever yet beheld. From that moment, her calm and self-possessed demeanor left her for ever. Abroad and at home, she was restless and uneasy. But, ere long, the stranger found an opportunity of being introduced to her, and mutual avowals of love followed at no great distance of time.

Assured of the affections of Elezia, the young stranger then presented himself to Mr. Baxwell. "I am named William Katt," said he to the merchant; "I am, like yourself, an Englishman; I am of respectable family and character, young, and wealthy. Give me your daughter — we love one another."

"Never!" said James Baxwell, to whom the position and circumstances of the young man were not unknown; "never! You belong to the denominant religion of England, by which my fathers suffered so much and so long. You are a Lutheran and my daughter is a Catholic. Such a union could not be happy; nor will I ever give my consent to it. Elezia shall never be yours!" The daughter, informed of this declaration, threw herself at the feet of her father, and endeavored to move him from his purpose. Her lover did the same. But the father remained obstinate, and a violent scene took place between Elezia and her parent. The blood of the fiery South coursed in the daughter's veins, and she declared that she *would* marry the object of her choice, despite of all opposition. James Baxwell, on the other hand, declared that he would sooner kill her with his own hands, than see her carry such a resolution into effect. As to William Katt, who stood by at this scene, he kept silence. What thoughts were revolving in his mind, it would be difficult to say.

Two days afterwards, an alarming noise was heard by the neighbors to issue from a cave immediately adjoining the merchant's house, and used by him for some domestic purposes. The noise consisted at first of loud cries, which gradually became fainter, and at length died altogether away. The auditors looked at each other with amazement, and many were the conjectures as to the cause of the sounds alluded to. A solution of the mystery was not long in suggesting itself. Elezia had disappeared; she was no longer to be seen about her father's house. After many low murmurs had circulated, the father was interrogated respecting his daughter. He said that she was missing, certainly; but whither she had gone, he knew not. He had nothing whatever to do, he said, with her disappearance.

This explanation was not satisfactory. The whisper went abroad that James Baxwell had assassinated his daughter, to prevent her marriage with William Katt, and, ultimately, this conjecture was so forcibly pressed on the attention of the public authorities, that they were compelled to arrest James Baxwell, and inquire into the matter. The dwelling of the merchant was examined, but nothing criminatory was found. "The cave! the cave is the place!" cried some of the crowd. The magistrates then descended into the cave, and there, on lifting some loose stones, they found a portion of Elezia's dress, sprinkled all over with blood. They also discovered a small quantity of hair, clotted with gore, and that hair was recognized by many as having been taken from the head of Elezia.

Baxwell protested his innocence. But the proof seemed strong against him, and he was regularly brought to trial. The result was his conviction for the murder of his daughter, and his condemnation to death.

On receiving sentence, the unhappy merchant trembled to excess, and afterwards seemed utterly overpowered by the dreadful nature of his situation. He continued in a state almost of total insensibility during the interval between his trial and the day appointed for his execution. On the morning of the latter day, the jailer came to announce to him, for the final time, that the moment was at hand. The merchant was seized again with a fearful trembling, and he cried, what he had reiterated to all who saw him in his confinement: "Before my Maker, I swear that I am guiltless of my child's death!"

They led him out to the scaffold. There he found, among others, William Katt, who, it should have been said, was the most important witness against him at his trial, having repeated to the court the threat of assassination which had been uttered by James Baxwell in his presence against Elezia. No sooner did the doomed merchant behold Katt, than he exclaimed, at the very foot of the scaffold: "My friend, in one minute I shall be in eternity. I wish to die in peace with all men. Give me your hand—I pardon you freely for the injury your evidence has done to me." Baxwell said this with some composure, but the effect of his words upon Katt were very striking. He became pale as death, and could not conceal the depth of his agitation.

Baxwell mounted the steps of the gallows slowly, and gave himself up to the hands of the executioner, to undergo death by the rope. According to the ancient custom of Gibraltar, the executioner commenced his last duties by crying in a loud voice: "Justice is doing! Justice is done!" He then placed the black bonnet on the head of the condemned merchant, and pulled it down in front, so as to cover the eyes. He had just done this, when he was stopped in his proceedings by a loud cry from the side of the scaffold: "*It is I who am guilty—I alone!*"

This cry came from William Katt. The magistrates in attendance instantly called him forward, and demanded an explanation. The young man avowed that he had carried off Elezia, with her consent, to be his wife, and that she was now residing not far off, in concealment. But to her he did not communicate other measures which he had taken, chiefly to revenge himself for the scorn of her father. He had contrived to cut off a portion of her hair while she slept. He had clotted it with the blood of a lamb, and had also sprinkled in the same way a part of Elezia's dress, which he had purloined. These articles he had placed in the cave, and there, also, had he emitted personally those cries which had borne so heavily against the merchant. The generous pardon which the merchant had bestowed on him at the scaffold, had awakened (the young man said) instantaneous remorse in his breast, and compelled him to avow the truth.

This confession was partly made at the scaffold, and partly afterwards. As soon as Katt had spoken out decisively, the executioner had turned to James Baxwell, to take from him the insignia of death. The merchant, almost unobserved, had sunk down into a sitting posture. The black bonnet was drawn by the executioner from off his eyes and head. It was found that he was a corpse! No exertions had the slightest effect in awakening in him the spark of life. The physicians, saying all they could on such a subject, declared that he had died from the effects of strong imagination.

William Katt was conducted to prison amid the clamors of the populace, there to await judgment for his misdeeds.

Elezia, the unhappy daughter of an unhappy father, retired to a convent for life immediately on learning all that had passed.

XX.

William Ridley kept the Red Cow, a public house at Exeter. John Miles was an old acquaintance of Ridley's, but they had not seen each other for some time (Miles living some distance off), when they met one morning, as the latter was going a little way to receive some money. They adjourned to the next public house, and, after drinking together, Ridley told Miles that he must go about the business which brought him from home, which was to receive a sum of money, but made him promise to wait for his coming back. Ridley returned, and they drank together again. Ridley now insisted upon Miles' accompanying him home to dinner. They dined, they drank, they shook hands, repeated old stories, drank and shook hands again and again, as old acquaintances in the lower class, after long absences, usually do; in fine, they both got, at last, pretty much in liquor.

The room they sat in was backwards, detached as it were from the house, with a door that went immediately into a yard, and had communication with the street, without passing through the house.

As it grew late, Mrs. Ridley came into the room, and not seeing her husband there, made inquiry after him of Miles. Miles being much intoxicated, all that could be got out of him was, that Ridley went out into the yard some time before, and had not returned. Ridley was called, Ridley was searched after, by all the family; but neither answering, nor being to be met with, Miles, as well as he was able for intoxication, went his way.

Ridley not coming home that night, and some days passing without his returning, or being heard of, suspicions arose, in the mind of Mrs. Ridley, of some foul play against her husband on the part of Miles; and these were not a little increased on the recollection that her husband had received a sum of money that day, and that Miles had replied to her inquiries after him in a very incoherent, unintelligible manner, which, at the time, she had attributed to his being in liquor.

These suspicions went abroad, and at length a full belief took place in many, that Miles was actually the murderer of Ridley; had gone out with him, robbed and murdered him, disposed of the body, and slid back again to the room where they were drinking, unseen by any one.

The officers of justice were sent to take up Miles,

and he giving, before the magistrate, a very unsatisfactory relation of his parting with Ridley, which he affirmed was owing to his having been intoxicated when Ridley went out of the room from him, but which the magistrate ascribed to guiltiness, he was committed to Exeter jail for trial.

Whilst Miles was in confinement, a thousand reports were spread, tending to warp the minds of the people against him. Supernatural as well as natural reasons were alleged as proof of his guilt. Ridley's house was declared to be haunted; frequent knockings were heard in the dead of the night; two of the lodgers avowed they had seen the ghost. And to crown the whole, an old man, another lodger, positively affirmed, that once, at midnight, his curtains flew open, the ghost of Ridley appeared, all bloody, and, with a piteous look and hollow voice, declared he had been murdered, and that Miles was the murderer.

Under these prepossessions amongst the weak and superstitious, and a general prejudice even in the stronger minds, was John Miles brought to trial for the willful murder of William Ridley. Circumstances upon circumstances were deposed against him; and as it appeared that Miles was with Ridley the whole day, both before and after his receiving the money, and that they spent the afternoon and evening together alone, the jury, who were neighbors of Ridley, found Miles guilty, notwithstanding his protestations, on his defense, of innocence, and he was shortly after executed at Exeter.

It happened, that, some time after, Mrs. Ridley left the Red Cow to keep another ale house, and the person who succeeded her, making several repairs in and about the house, in emptying the necessary, which was at the end of a long dark passage, the body of William Ridley was discovered. In his pockets were found twenty guineas, from whence it was evident he had not been murdered, as the robbing of him was the sole circumstance that could be and was ascribed to Miles for murdering of Ridley. The truth of Miles' assertions and defense now became doubly evident; for it was recollected that the floor of the necessary had been taken up the morning before the death of Ridley, and that, on one side of the seat, a couple of boards had been left up; so that, being much in liquor, he must have fallen into the vault, which was uncommonly deep; but which, unhappily, was not adverted to at the time of his disappearance!

XXI.

Two men were seen fighting together in a field. One of them was found, soon after, lying dead in that field. Near him lay a pitchfork which had apparently been the instrument of his death. This pitchfork was known to have belonged to the person who had been seen fighting with the deceased; and he was known to have taken it out with him that morning. Being apprehended and brought to trial, and these circumstances appearing in evidence, and also that there had been, for some time, an enmity between the parties, there was little doubt of the prisoner's being convicted, although he strongly persisted in his innocence; but, to the great surprise of the court, the jury, instead of bringing in an immediate verdict of guilty, withdrew, and, after staying out a considerable time, returned and informed the court, that eleven, out of the twelve, had been, from the first, for finding the prisoner guilty; but that one man would not concur in the verdict. Upon this, the judge observed to the dissentient person, the great strength of the circumstances, and asked him, "how it was possible, *all circumstances con-*

sidered, for him to have any doubts of the guilt of the accused?" But no arguments that could be urged, either by the court or the rest of the jury, could persuade him to find the prisoner guilty; so that the rest of the jury were at last obliged to agree to the verdict of acquittal.

This affair remained, for some time, mysterious; but it at length came out, either by the private acknowledgment of the obstinate juryman to the judge who tried the cause (who is said to have had the curiosity to inquire into the motives of his extraordinary pertinacity), or by his confession at the point of death (for the case is related both ways), that he himself had been the murderer! The accused had, indeed, had a scuffle with the deceased, as sworn on the trial, in which he had dropped his pitchfork, which had been, soon after, found by the juryman, between whom and the deceased an accidental quarrel had arisen in the same field; the deceased having continued there at work after the departure of the person with whom he had been seen to have the affray; in the heat of which quarrel, the juryman had unfortunately stabbed him with that very pitchfork, and had then got away totally unsuspected; but finding, soon after, that the other person had been apprehended, on suspicion of being the murderer, and fearing, as the circumstances appeared so strong against him, that he should be convicted, although not guilty, he had contrived to get upon the jury, as the only way of saving the innocent without endangering himself.

XXII.

John Hawkins and George Simpson were indicted for robbing the mail, on the 16th of April, 1722. Hawkins, in his defense, set up an *alibi*, to prove which, he called one William Fuller, who deposed, that Hawkins came to his house on Sunday, the 15th of April, and lay there that night, and did not go out until the next morning. Being asked by the court, "By what token do you remember that it was the 15th* of April?" he replied, "By a very good token, for he owed me a sum of money for horse hire, and on Tuesday, the 10th of April, he called upon me and paid me in full, and I gave him a receipt; and I very well remember, that he lay at my house the Sunday night following." The receipt was now produced. "April the 10th, 1722. Received of Mr. John Hawkins, the sum of one pound ten shillings, in full of all accounts, per me, William Fuller." Upon inspecting the receipt, the court asked Fuller who wrote it. He replied, "Hawkins wrote the body of it, and I signed it."

* The robbery was committed about two o'clock on the morning of the 16th.

Court. "Did you see him write it?"

Fuller. "Yes."

Court. "And how long was it after he wrote it, before you signed?"

Fuller. "I signed it immediately, without going from the table."

Court. "How many standishes do you keep in the house?"

Fuller. "Standishes?"

Court. "Aye, standishes · it is a plain question."

Fuller. "My Lord, but one; and that is enough for the little handwriting we have to do."

Court. "Then you signed the receipt with the same ink that Hawkins wrote the body of it with?"

Fuller. "For certain."

Court. "Officer, hand the receipt to the jury. Gentlemen, you will see that the body of the note is written with one kind of ink, and the name at the bottom with another very different; and yet this witness has sworn, that they were both written with the same ink, and one immediately after the other. You will judge what credit is to be given to his evidence!"

Thus, the authenticity of the receipt, and the credit of the witness, were overthrown by the sagacity of the court! But while the judge, Lord Chief Baron MONTAGUE was summing up the evidence, he was interrupted by the following occurrence: The person who reports the trial was then taking notes of the proceedings; his ink, as it happened, was very bad, being thick at the bottom, and thin and waterish at the top, so that, accordingly as he dipped the pen, the writing appeared very pale or pretty black. This circumstance being remarked by some gentlemen present, they handed the book to the jury; the judge perceiving them very attentively inspecting it, called to them: "Gentlemen, what are you doing? What book is that?" They told him that it was the writer's book, and that they were observing how the same ink appeared pale in one place, and black in another. The judge then told them—"You ought not, gentlemen to take notice of any thing but what is produced in evidence"; and, turning to the writer, demanded—"what he meant by showing that book to the jury?" And being informed by the writer that it was taken from him, he inquired "who took it, and who handed it to the jury?" But this the writer could not say, as the gentlemen near him were all strangers to him, and he had not taken any particular notice of the person who took his book.

That a jury ought not to take notice of any thing but what is produced in evidence, has been said to be law; but, on the contrary, it has been held, and surely very properly, that a juryman may find from his own knowledge; indeed, what evidence can convince a person that *is* which he knows *not* to be?

Hawkins and Simpson were convicted and executed; indeed, the evidence against them was very strong; but, had the fate of Hawkins depended upon the single testimony of Fuller, he would, but for this occurrence, have fallen a sacrifice to the acuteness of the judge! who appears to have been much displeased at the accidental confutation of his remarks on the receipt, although it was an accident in favor of life; and, had it not been in a case where other evidence was so strong against the accused, it must have been looked upon as the special interposition of Providence.

XXIII.

A MAN was tried for, and convicted of, the murder of his own father. The evidence against him was merely circumstantial, and the principal witness was his sister. She proved that her father possessed a small income, which, with his industry, enabled him to live with comfort; that her brother, the prisoner, who was his heir at law, had long expressed a great desire to come into the possession of his father's effects; and that he had long behaved in a very undutiful manner to him, wishing, as the witness believed, to put a period to his existence by uneasiness and vexation; that, on the evening the murder was committed, the deceased went a small distance from the house, to milk a cow he had for some time kept, and that the witness also went out to spend the evening and to sleep, leaving only her brother in the house; that, returning home early in the morning, and finding that her father and brother were absent, she was much alarmed, and sent for some neighbors to consult with them, and to receive advice what should be done; that, in company with these neighbors, she went to the hovel in which her father was accustomed to milk the cow, where they found him murdered in an inhuman manner, his head being almost beat to pieces; that a suspicion immediately falling on her brother, and there being then some snow upon the ground, in which the footsteps of a human being, to and from the hovel, were observed, it was agreed to take one of the brother's shoes, and to measure therewith the impressions in the snow; this was done, and there did not remain a doubt but that the impressions were made with his shoes. Thus confirmed in their suspicions, they then immediately went to the prisoner's room, and after a diligent search, they found a hammer, in the corner of a private drawer, with several spots of blood upon it, and with a small splinter of bone, and some brains in a crack which they discovered in the handle. The circumstances of finding the deceased and the hammer, as described by the former witness, were fully proved by the neighbors whom she had called; and upon this evidence the prisoner was convicted and suffered death, but denied the fact to the last. About four years after, the witness was extremely ill, and understanding that there were no possible hopes of her recovery, she confessed that her father and brother having offended her, she was determined they should both die ; and, accordingly, when the former went to milk the cow, she followed him with her brother's hammer, and in his shoes; that she beat out her father's brains with the hammer, and laid it where it was afterwards found ; that she then went from home to give a better color to this wicked business, and that her brother was perfectly innocent of the crime for which he had suffered. She was immediately taken into custody, but died before she could be brought to trial.

XXIV.

John Stringer was tried at the Lent assizes, held at Kingston, in the county of Surry, in the year 1765, before the late Lord Chief Baron Smythe, for the murder of his wife, and found guilty. The trial being on the Saturday, he was ordered for execution on the Monday following. The case was thus: Stringer, a man in low circumstances, had brought his wife, who had long been in an ill state of health, from London to Lambeth, for the benefit of the air; here they lived for some time; generally in great harmony; but not without those little quarrels and scuffles, so common with persons in their rank of life. Upon the woman's death, some of the neighboring females, who had been occasionally witnesses to these litttle accidental bickerings between the husband and wife, took it in their heads that he had murdered her, notwithstanding she had never been heard to make the least complaint of her husband during the course of her illness; and the man was brought to trial in consequence.

Some trifling evidence being given of the little

differences that had arisen between them; and the opinion of a young surgeon, that some appearances on the corpse were somewhat the appearances of a mortification, occasioned by bruises; Stringer, on these slight circumstances, was convicted, and left for execution!

Mr. Carsan, a surgeon of great experience in the neighborhood, had, on the report of the murder, from mere curiosity, examined the body, and was so clear that there were no marks of violence thereon, that he had not the least apprehension of the possibility of Stringer's being convicted: but hearing of the conviction, and confident of the innocence of the unhappy man, and actuated by the love of justice and humanity, he instantly, on the Sunday, waited on, and represented the case to the Archbishop of Canterbury; his grace gave Mr. Carsan a letter to Baron SMYTHE, who, convinced by his statement of the matter, that himself and the jury had been too precipitate in forming an opinion of the guilt of Stringer, granted an immediate respite; which gave Mr. Carsan an opportunity of laying the whole case before his majesty, and he had the satisfaction of saving an innocent man from an undeserved and ignominious death.

XXV.

In the year 1764, a citizen of Liege was found dead in his chamber, shot in the head. Close to him lay a discharged pistol, with which he had apparently been his own executioner. Firearms are the chief manufacture of that city; and so common is the use of pistols at that place, that every peasant, who brings his goods to the markets there, is seen armed with them; so that the circumstance of the pistol did not, at first, meet with so much attention as it might have done in places where those weapons are not in such common use. But, upon the researches of the proper officer of that city, whose duty, like that of our coroner, it is to inquire into all the circumstances of accidental deaths, it appeared that the ball which was found lodged in the head of the deceased could never, from its size, have been fired out of the pistol which lay by him; thus it was clear that he had been murdered; nor were they long in deciding who was the murderer. A girl, of about sixteen, the niece of the deceased, had been brought up by him, and he had been always supposed to have intended to leave her his effects, which were something considerable; but the girl had then lately listened to the addresses of a young man whom the uncle did not approve of, and he had, upon that occasion, several times threatened to alter his will, and leave his fortune to some other of his relations. Upon these, and some other concurrent circumstances, such as having been heard to wish her uncle's death, &c., the girl was committed to prison.

The torturing a supposed criminal, in order to force confession, is certainly the most cruel and absurd idea that ever entered into the head of a legislator. This being observed by the writer of this narrative, who was then at Liege, to a magistrate of that place, on this very occasion, his defense was,—"We never condemn to the torture but upon circumstances on which you in England would convict; so that the innocent has really a better chance to escape here than with you." But, until it is proved that pain has a greater tendency to make a person speak truth than falsehood, this reasoning seems to have little weight.

This unhappy girl was, therefore, horridly and repeatedly tortured; but still persevering in asserting her innocence, she at last escaped with life;—if it could be called an escape, when it was supposed she would never again enjoy health or limbs, from the effects of the torture.

The writer has since learned, that, some years afterwards, her innocence became manifest, by the confession of the real assassins, who, being sentenced to the wheel for other crimes, confessed themselves the authors of this of which the girl was suspected; and that, several pistols having been discharged at the deceased, they had, intending that it should appear a suicide, laid a pistol near him, without adverting that it was not the same by which he fell.

XXVI.

Jonathan Bradford kept an inn, in Oxfordshire, on the London road to Oxford. He bore a very unexceptionable character. Mr. Hayes, a gentleman of fortune, being on his way to Oxford, on a visit to a relation, put up at Bradford's. He there joined company with two gentlemen, with whom he supped, and, in conversation, unguardedly mentioned that he had then about him a sum of money. In due time they retired to their respective chambers; the gentlemen to a two-bedded room, leaving, as is customary with many, a candle burning in the chimney corner. Some hours after they were in bed, one of the gentlemen, being awake, thought he heard a deep groan in an adjoining chamber; and this being repeated, he softly awaked his friend. They listened together, and the groans increasing, as of one dying and in pain, they both instantly arose, and proceeded silently to the door of the next chamber, whence they bad heard the groans, and, the door being ajar, saw a light in the room. They entered, but it is impossible to paint their consternation, on perceiving a person weltering in his blood in the bed, and a man standing over him with a dark lantern in one hand, and a knife in the other! The man seemed as petrified as themselves, but his terror carried with it all the terror of guilt. The gentlemen soon discovered that the murdered person was the stranger with whom they had that night supped, and that the man who was standing over him was their host. They seized Bradford directly, disarmed him of his knife, and charged him with being the murderer. He assumed, by this time, the air of innocence, positively denied the crime, and asserted that he came there with the same humane intentions as themselves; for that, hearing a noise, which was succeeded by a groaning, he got out of bed, struck a light, armed himself with a knife for his defense, and was but that minute entered the room before them. These assertions were of little avail; he was kept in close custody till the morning, and then taken before a neighboring justice of the peace. Bradford still denied the murder, but, nevertheless, with such apparent indications of guilt, that the justice hesitated not to make use of this most extraordinary expression, on writing out his mittimus: "Mr. Bradford, either you or myself committed this murder."

This extraordinary affair was the conversation of the whole country. Bradford was tried and condemned, over and over again, in every company. In the midst of all this predetermination, came on the assizes at Oxford. Bradford was brought to trial; he pleaded—not guilty. Nothing could be stronger than the evidence of the two gentlemen. They testified to the finding Mr. Hayes murdered in his bed; Bradford at the side of the body with a light and a knife; that knife, and the hand which held it, bloody; that, on their entering the room, he betrayed all the signs of a guilty man; and that, but a few moments preceding, they had heard the groans of the deceased.

Bradford's defense on his trial was the same as before the gentlemen: he had heard a noise; he suspected some villany was transacting; he struck a light; he snatched the knife, the only weapon near him, to defend himself; and the terrors he discovered were merely the terrors of humanity, the natural effects of innocence as well as guilt, on beholding such a horrid scene.

This defense, however, could not be considered but as weak, contrasted with the several powerful circumstances against him. Never was circumstantial evidence more strong! There was little need of the prejudice of the county against the murderer to strengthen it; there was little need left of comment from the judge, in summing up the evidence; no room appeared for extenuation; and the jury brought in the prisoner guilty, even without going out of their box.

Bradford was executed shortly after, still declaring that he was not the murderer, nor privy to the murder of Mr. Hayes; but he died disbelieved by all.

Yet were these assertions not untrue! The murder was actually committed by Mr. Hayes' footman; who, immediately on stabbing his master, rifled his breeches of his money, gold watch, and snuff-box, and escaped back to his own room; which could have been, from the after circumstances, scarcely two seconds before Bradford's entering the unfortunate gentleman's chamber. The world owes this knowledge to a remorse of conscience in the footman (eighteen months after the execution of Bradford), on a bed of sickness. It was a death-bed repentance, and by that death the law lost its victim.

It is much to be wished that this account could close here,—but it cannot! Bradford, though innocent, and not privy to the murder, was, nevertheless, the murderer in design: he had heard, as well as the footman, what Mr. Hayes declared at supper, as to the having a sum of money about him; and he went to the chamber of the deceased with the same diabolical intentions as the servant. He was struck with amazement; he could not believe his senses; and, in turning back the bed-clothes, to assure himself of the fact, he, in his agitation, dropped his knife on the bleeding body, by which both his hands and the knife became bloody. These circumstances Bradford acknowledged to the clergyman who attended him after his sentence.

XXVII.

THE most remarkable murder trial which Boston has seen since the famous Webster-Parkman case, was that which resulted in a verdict that Leavitt Alley was not guilty of the murder of Abijah Ellis. There is at many points a wonderful parallelism in the two trials. The victims were both men of wealth, and of strikingly similar habits ; both were hard creditors, and the incentive alleged in each case was the inability of the murderer to meet a certain payment. The horrible circumstances attending the finding of Ellis's body—just after the mysterious shooting of Charles Lane, a wealthy merchant, in his own doorway—and the consequent excitement, equaled in intensity only by the discovery of the charred remains of Dr. Parkman, a score of years before, will serve to recall the salient features of the case.

Some workmen near the Cambridge gas works, discovered two barrels, containing the mutilated body, floating in the Charles river. They were packed with horse manure and shavings, and in one of the barrels was discovered a piece of brown paper with the name of M. Schouler, a billiard manufacturer. Investigation proved that a teamster, Leavitt Alley, was in the habit of removing these shavings to his stable. Following the clew to the stable, it was found that a dry manure heap had been recently disturbed ; blood was also found upon some boards near by.

It was proved that on the previous morning Alley had started from his stable with four barrels, and a teamster, in jumping from the wagon, had ascertained that two of them were heavy. Two of the barrels were not satisfactorily accounted for, while a man testified to seeing the team and barrels with a man strongly resembling Alley upon the mill-dam, where they were supposed to have been thrown into the river. Alley was owing Ellis some two hundred dollars, was in great need of money, and Ellis was known to have been searching for the suspected man on the night when the murder was probably committed. A new axe which Alley had purchased a short time before was missing, and its very existence was denied. In addition, blood stains were found upon the clothing worn by Alley, which were identified by experts as human gore ; and a woman had heard strange noises, like the rolling of barrels, in the stable on the fatal night. Lastly, it was shown that Alley had been abundantly provided with money after the death of Ellis.

The testimony for the government was entirely circumstantial. It was not claimed that any human eye saw, or human ear heard, the doing of the atrocious deed. The case had been carefully worked up and prepared by the best detective skill and professional ability that could be brought to bear upon it, and, as the facts already given were clearly brought out, the outlook for the prisoner was certainly a dark one as compared with the Webster trial, when the whole case turned upon the identification by a dentist of a gold plate. The stains of blood found in the prisoner's stable and on his clothing were submitted to chemical tests, by skillful experts, and then examined through a microscope, and pronounced by them to be not only human blood, but that of the murdered man. A physician testified, from an examination of the deceased's stomach, that he must have met his death between six and nine o'clock on the fatal evening; and altogether the case against Alley was about as strong a one as circumstantial evidence ever presents.

The prisoner's counsel, however, appeared to fully appreciate the situation, and developed an unexpected strength. To controvert the theory that Alley had committed the murder in a quarrel, they introduced evidence from prominent citizens of New Hampshire that he had always been a quiet and peaceable man, with a reputation for honesty and integrity above reproach, in the face of which the commission of so horrible a crime seemed most unlikely. The prosecution had claimed that Alley was in debt to Ellis, and without money to meet an engagement which fell due at the time of the murder; but the defense clearly proved that the prisoner possessed considerable property in New Hampshire and had money in a bank.

A strong point against the accused had been the fact that, though he had not much ready money on hand just before the murder, immediately after it he had considerable in his possession. But the defense disposed of this by evidence that a loan of one hundred and twenty-five dollars was repaid by his son the evening before the murder. There remained the evidence of the blood, which the prosecution had professed to prove was not only human blood, but that of the victim himself. But the defense introduced experts, who not only denied that the blood in question was that of a human being, but showed that the best scientific authorities agree that the difference between human and animal blood cannot be determined after it has dried, as was the fact in this case.

On the whole, therefore, the scientific testimony not only served to confuse the jury, but positively helped the prisoner's case. The defense then proceeded to still further dissipate the web of circumstantial evidence which had been woven around Alley by satisfactorily accounting for every hour of his time from the moment Ellis disappeared till the time his body was discovered.

When the defense rested their case, public opinion and expectation had naturally, and justly, very much changed, and the probability of his conviction had practically disappeared. No one had seen the murder, and the natural indisposition to condemn a man on circumstantial evidence alone was strengthened by the fact that much of what appeared strongest in this evidence had been overthrown by the defense. These considerations, joined with the traditional principle of holding every man innocent till his guilt is proved beyond the shadow of a doubt, resulted in a verdict of not guilty—a decision of the case with which the public will not be inclined to find fault.

www.ingramcontent.com/pod-product-compliance
Lightning Source LLC
LaVergne TN
LVHW010742120826
845150LV00009B/1401